Bletchley Park People

CHURCHILL'S 'GEESE THAT NEVER CACKLED'

MARION HILL

6

SUTTON PUBLISHING

First published in the United Kingdom in 2004 by
Sutton Publishing Limited · Phoenix Mill
Thrupp · Stroud · Gloucestershire · GL5 2BU

British Library Cataloguing in Publication Data
A catalogue record for this book is available from the British Library.

ISBN 0-7509-3362-3

Typeset in 11/12 pt Ehrhardt MT.
Typesetting and origination by
Sutton Publishing Limited.
Printed in Great Britain by
J.H. Haynes & Co., Ltd, Sparkford, England.

Contents

	Author's Note	4
	Foreword	5
	Prologue	6
1	The Bletchley Park Estate	7
2	Recruitment and Training of the 'Geese'	13
3	First Impressions	24
4	Where the 'Geese' Worked	30
5	What the 'Geese' Did	35
6	Working Conditions	49
7	Boffins and Debs	62
8	Service Personnel	72
9	The Civilian Division	85
10	Food and Entertainment	88
11	Billets and Beyond	104
12	The Intercept Stations and Outstations	122
13	Concerns and Regrets	128
	Epilogue	136
	Notes	137
	Sources and Acknowledgements	137

Author's note

This book includes verbatim extracts, most of them stored in the Bletchley Park Trust Archive (BPTA), from over 200 former workers at Bletchley Park during the Second World War. Many accounts have been amalgamated to create a composite picture of what life was like then. For this reason individual acknowledgement of extracts is the exception (for specific events only) rather than the rule. A full list of sources can be found at the back of the book.

Foreword

In 1991, the Bletchley Park site was empty and plans were afoot to demolish all the buildings to make way for a housing development. That spring the Bletchley Archaeological and Historical Society formed a small committee to bring together as many former code-breakers as could be traced for a farewell 'thank you' before the site was destroyed. On 21 October 1991, the farewell party was held in the grounds with over 400 people attending. As a result of the stories they told, it was decided to attempt the restoration of the site for posterity. The Bletchley Park Trust grew from this small committee.

Today the trust comprises a Board of Trustees who, together with employees and volunteers, are operating the site and planning major redevelopment. The essence of this plan is to preserve and consolidate the historic aspects of the Park while at the same time securing its long-term sustainability and viability by innovative enhancement.

The 'BP' of the future will celebrate the development and impact of Second World War intelligence work, computing and cryptography by creating a campus dedicated to the science of communication. On site are the world's only reconstructed and working Colossus and Tunny machines. A Turing Bombe is being rebuilt using the original blueprints. A reconstruction of the original intercept station in the tower at the top of the house has been completed.

However, the future of the Park is not only about sharing the site's amazing history. It is to be a living site contributing to the 'now' as well as celebrating the 'then' – a 'newseum', not just a museum. To this end the Trust is creating alliances with leaders in telecommunications, computing, media, education and leisure as well as community groups. Long-term plans include: a visitors' centre; a purpose-built Education Centre housing the Alan Turing Academy for talented young students; an Enigma Studio for visiting schoolchildren; and dedicated trails.

The stories in this book are testament to the dedication and diligence of thousands of Bletchley Park workers during the last war. It is an honour for the Trust to support their publication and thereby celebrate the remarkable phenomenon that was BP.

Christine Large
Chief Executive of Bletchley Park Trust

Prologue

'The most amazing thing to me always will be that nearly 10,000 people
in BP never blabbed one single word about this operation.'

In 1939, 'Room 47' at the Foreign Office had been a secret team of people set up
after the First World War to decipher coded messages from abroad. When war
broke out, the team – ninety strong – was transferred to Bletchley Park, or BP as
it was subsequently known. By 1945, their numbers had increased one
hundredfold.[1] Over a third of them were civilians and three-quarters were
women. When, at the end of the war, BP machinery was summarily dismantled,
its materials burned and shredded, what went on there was still a secret. It
remained so for thirty years.

At its height, up to 5,000 coded messages were received daily at BP from
listening stations all over the country. The Germans' coding machine, Enigma,
could put a message into code in over 15 million billion ways; and they would
change the settings every twenty-four hours. Looking like a bulky old-fashioned
typewriter, the Enigma machine had variations of 17,576 alphabets; and changing
the wiring created a total of permutations that started with the figure 5 followed
by 92 noughts.

The seemingly impossible task of breaking Enigma was eventually
accomplished. This book is not about how that happened. It is not about the
intricate decoding systems, nor the technical data of Britain's first computers like
the 'Bombes' and 'Colossus', nor the genius methods employed by the best brains
of Britain. Here instead are the personal stories of people who worked at
Bletchley Park from 1938 to 1945, the people who in Churchill's words were 'the
geese who laid the golden egg and never cackled'. They give 'a human account of
what life in the Park was like for six years of war – indeed what life was like
outside the rarefied atmosphere of BP'.

Above all, this book is about the phenomenon of secrecy that was Bletchley
Park. It is dedicated to the people who resolutely safeguarded its secret for so
long, and whose subsequent reminiscences are now such a valuable historical
resource.

Marion Hill

CHAPTER 1

The Bletchley Park Estate

'Illustrated Particulars, Plan and Conditions of Sale
of the
Important Freehold, Residential, Agricultural & Building Property known as the
BLETCHLEY PARK ESTATE'[2]

As the new year of 1937 began, just a month after the sensational abdication of King Edward VIII, Fanny, Lady Leon lay dying in her Bletchley Park mansion. It had been her home for fifty-five years.

Perhaps she was still able to see from the large bay window in her bedroom some of the forty-four acres of parkland. Here in its heyday forty gardeners had tended the ornamental trees, the yew-tree maze, the walled kitchen garden and the lake shaded by trees and bounded by rockeries and shrubs. Perhaps her mind wandered back to summer days of leather-on-willow when locals played cricket on a first-class pitch just beyond the tennis courts. She would host tea in the elegant pavilion; her husband would show off his special prize-winning breed of

The main entrance to the mansion, c. 1924. (BPTA 44.vi)

Fanny, Lady Leon at her desk in the mansion at Bletchley Park, c. 1935. (BPTA P96.7)

shorthorn cattle, or the latest delight in their two orchid houses, or the products of the Peach and Apricot Houses.

Perhaps her thoughts might have dwelt on her long-dead husband – Sammy as she knew him, Sir Herbert Leon 1st Baronet as he was known in formal circles. It had been a fortuitous marriage: Sammy had been born into, and nurtured, a vast fortune. He had become head of the family firm of stockbrokers (Leon Brothers of Throgmorton Street) and 'made a profession out of being wealthy', as evidenced by his two Rolls Royces. Yet he was considered to be an extraordinarily generous man. Together they had sponsored local events of all kinds at Bletchley Park including horse-jumping and fireworks displays. Out of this had grown the annual Bletchley Show, the first in 1914 attracting around 5,000 people. It must have been gratifying for Fanny to recall the last one just six months ago in the summer of 1936, when nearly three times that number had attended, even though it was nine years after Sammy's death.

Perhaps, too, she mused on all those demands on his time and energies. As well as running the family business, Sammy had been Liberal MP for Buckinghamshire, Chairman of the Bletchley Urban District Council, High Sheriff of Buckinghamshire and a Justice of the Peace. He had held Directorships of the Anglo-American Telegraph Company and the Daily News; and of the company running the largest steam tram in the world, the Wolverton Tram Company, shuttling 4,000 workers between Stony Stratford and the huge

Wolverton Railway Works. His close friend Lloyd George had been a frequent visitor to Bletchley Park – indeed the mansion and grounds were willingly made available for the Liberal Party rally. After Sammy had been nominated by Prime Minister Asquith, and selected, to become a baronet in 1911, their friends came from even higher places: they hunted at Whaddon Chase with the Prince of Wales and the Duke of York.

In those final days as Fanny languished, she might have been comforted by the familiar room around her, gazing on its elaborately carved wood and glazed mantelpiece, and its ornate ceiling, or looking through into its adjacent bathroom resplendent with nickel-plated bath, marble-topped lavatory and heated towel rails. For she and Sammy had created this place. They had built and furnished it from practically nothing. Despite mention of its land in the Domesday Book, and previous illustrious owners like the Duke of Buckingham, Bletchley Park had for centuries been an unremarkable property. She and Sammy had changed all that.

Fanny had arrived with her new husband in 1882; a year later they had enlarged and improved the house beyond recognition. Construction materials had been brought by canal barge, unloaded at Fenny Wharf, then transported to the Park by horse and cart. The pillars at the entrance had come at great expense from Italy, but they befitted what lay beyond, the grandeur Sir Herbert and Lady

The dining room, pictured in the sale particulars from 1937. (BPTA P94.15.11)

Leon enjoyed. There was a suite of four oak-panelled reception rooms – the dining room, drawing room, morning room and library; and there was a billiard room, a conservatory and a magnificent ballroom. There were twenty-seven bedrooms, eighteen of them with dressing rooms. There were seven bathrooms, and central heating and electric lights throughout from their own generator. They even had their own laundry room. Theirs was a very modern mansion.

Outside there were further examples of contemporary living: the old Squash Racquet court had been converted to a garage for three cars, and there was a cycle house as well as stables for at least a dozen horses. Staff had been well provided for too – up to 200 of them at one time – from three-bedroomed cottages for the stud groom, the head gardener and the engineer to loft-rooms for the stable lads, workshops for the plumber and carpenter, and offices for the butler and housekeeper.

Fanny, Lady Leon died on 23 January 1937. With her died Bletchley Park's period of provincial gentility. Its next era produced the stuff of legends . . .

On Wednesday, 28 July 1937, at 3 p.m., the old Leon Estate – now advertised as the Bletchley Park Estate – came under the hammer. Messrs Knight, Frank & Rutley of Hanover Square (in conjunction with Messrs Whatley, Hill & Co of St James') had been instructed by Sir George Leon, heir to the family fortune, to dispose of the freehold of all 581 acres and numerous buildings of the estate at the highest possible price. With just six months elapsed after his stepmother's death, Sir George had no interest in assuming the trappings of a country squire, nor in continuing any dynastic tradition in Bletchley. He was happy instead for the auctioneers to promote the sale, in sixteen lots, as 'Important Freehold, Residential, Agricultural and Building Property'. All this, declared the sale particulars, was situated at 'the important Railway Junction on the London Midland & Scottish Main Line from London to Rugby, Birmingham, Crewe and the North, and adjoined the Railway Station for Bedford and Oxford'. It had, moreover, 'nearly a mile frontage on the north-east to the main Birmingham Road (Watling Street)' with 'main Drainage' and the potential for factory development. Notwithstanding its modern attributes, the estate was in addition, 'exceptionally well placed in an important Hunting district . . . in the centre of the Whaddon Chase, whose kennels are close by, and [with] the Duke of Grafton's, Bicester and Oakley Hunts . . . all within easy reach'. Perhaps it was a combination of both these potential assets – aristocratic sport and business profit – that attracted a consortium of developers led by a local man, Captain Hubert Faulkner. They successfully bid for Lot 1: Bletchley Park's house and grounds.

By the beginning of 1938, many changes had been made to the property. Captain Faulkner had already demolished one wing in the Stable Yard, and converted others to cottages and flats. He reportedly intended also to demolish the house and other buildings, build a new mansion down by the lake and sell the land as a housing site. However, 'Captain Faulkner was approached by Government agents representing a branch of the Foreign Office, the Government and Code and Cypher School (GC&CS) . . . looking for a quiet country retreat from which to carry on its Foreign Office duties'.[3] Bletchley Park was readily

Bletchley Park Stables and buildings, 1937. (BPTA P94.15.6)

available, had a large telephone cable running nearby through the Fenny Stratford GPO repeater station, and had excellent road and rail links both for London and the North, and from Oxford and Cambridge.

A child of the times, Winifred Hymers, recalled what happened next: 'In the spring of 1938, my father Harry Hymers went to BP [Bletchley Park] with his boss Captain Ridley to get the place ready in case of a "National Emergency". He had a camp bed and a kettle and slept in the big house. He came home most weekends, and ate some of his meals in The Eight Bells. The family moved into No 2 Cottage, Stable Yard, in July.'

The Hymers family were to reside there for the next four years, but had initial problems in their new home. Captain Faulkner was retained for a while as a sort of site manager to deal with them: 'The loft space was very dirty and there were only two bedrooms on the ground floor. My parents explained to Mr Faulkner they needed three. He drew a line on the floor of the bedroom on the left of the front door which had two sash windows. The partition was hastily built at such a strange angle that we could only conclude the men had built it on the pencil mark. [There were] constant power cuts, problems with the water supply, and the water was often a dirty brown colour.' In September 1938, when Winifred's family had been joined on the site by around 200 people 'as a rehearsal', she recalled a wooden fence being erected around the perimeter. She also remembered being allowed to go in the big house when no people were around: 'There were grand fireplaces, ornate ceilings, and fluted pillars in the ballroom. Upstairs there were two grand lavatories whose bowls were willow pattern.'

The ballroom, 1937, soon to be part of the headquarters of GCCS – the Government Code and Cypher School, the forerunner of GCHQ in Cheltenham. (BPTA P94.15.12)

The House was invaded by new arrivals. The Security Intelligence Service (SIS) moved into the upper floor; GCCS moved into the ground floor with its head, Commander Denniston. The Park was ready for its new function: it was given the cover name 'Station X', a gloriously mysterious designation which actually had quite a prosaic origin: it was the tenth of a large number of sites acquired by MI6 for its wartime operations.[4] And it was unarguably to become its most significant weapon in the secret war and, ultimately, its most famous success. The gaggle of 'geese' who would effect this – the thousands of people who worked at BP over the next seven years – was about to gather.

CHAPTER 2

Recruitment and Training of the 'Geese'

'Memo to Mr De Grey[5] – immediate personnel for Hut 3: I suggest that 15 people be asked for at once. As you know I have already approached Pembroke College Oxford and they have promised to send me some names in a few weeks' time.'[6]

The recruitment drive for 'Station X' had to be a subtle affair. Its top-secret function could not allow job advertisements. But informal networks already operating in the Establishment could be exploited: the Services, universities and professions were shot through with those who were known and trusted, especially needed at this time of national emergency. Family connections were a safe start.

For example, if your father was the Brigadier in charge of 'Y Service' – the 'listening stations' supplying Bletchley Park with enemy codes to decipher – then perhaps it was unsurprising 'to find oneself working at BP when I was just 18'. The father of another BP worker, a Major from the First World War's Royal Flying Corps, became the Quartering Officer for the placement of troops. He was also able to deal with the placement of his daughter at BP, this occurring, she writes, 'during my last term of boarding school at Cheltenham Ladies College'.

All able-bodied men and women were expected to perform war work in the circumscribed society that was wartime Britain, but there were choices. For women, for example, it could be the WAAFs (Women's Auxiliary Air Force), WAACs (Women's Army Auxiliary Corps), WRNS (Women's Royal Naval Service), the ATS (Auxiliary Territorial Service), the Land Army (women who did farm work) or the FO (Foreign Office). The Major's daughter referred to above was promptly accepted in the latter with instructions 'to take a train to Bletchley, Bucks, phone this number and ask for transportation'.

Other useful relations included the Head of the Japanese section at BP: 'I wrote to [him] to ask if there might be a job for me at Bletchley. He rang up and said, Come as fast as you can . . . I alighted at Bletchley Station and was there met by my dear cousin, tall, very thin, with a straggling reddish beard and madder-looking than ever. . .'. This was Hugh Foss,[7] renowned for his 'very elegant' Scottish Country Dancing and immortalised in a contemporary ditty:

'F is for Foss 6ft 6 in his shoes,
Seen in a kilt, but not tartan trews
If on a Friday a stroll you will take
You'll find him dancing a reel by the lake.'

However, some BP workers took a dim view of family connections, especially if they seemed to nurture favouritism. One worked for 'Mr Freeborn[8] who I presumed was someone quite big in Hollerith.[9] His two sons were here as well, which got my back up as they were of military age and they were in charge of various sections here.'

Because the nature of the work developing at Bletchley Park required special brainpower, which known families could not always provide, the search had to be nationwide. A meeting held at BP on 23 March 1942 acknowledged that recruitment for its secret and complex work had to be radical if it was to assemble the 'right' people: 'Colonel Nicholls hoped that a line of country that he was exploring might help as regards cryptographic personnel, namely getting hold of people who had been regular competitors in *Daily Telegraph* Crossword Competitions and the like.'

On 15 January 1942, would-be recruits were challenged to complete a crossword within twelve minutes for a *Daily Telegraph* competition. One still had a clue to solve at the end of the allotted time, yet several weeks later was summoned 'to see Colonel Nicholls of the General Staff on a confidential matter of national importance . . . I reported to No 1 Albany Road, Bedford – the "Spy School" – on 3rd August 1942. I was [then] called up from the school for an interview at Devonshire House.'[10]

Unfortunately, such competitions harvested only a handful of recruits. Soon, potential 'geese' were deemed suitable if, when prompted, they merely expressed an interest: 'I was the only one of our intake who came to BP because they asked for hobbies and I put down crosswords.'

However, Colonel Nicholls was exploring another 'line of country . . . getting in touch with Headmasters of Public Schools . . . trying to get suitable boys as soon as they left school.'[11] Certainly a few recruits were trawled from male public school-leavers in this way: 'I got an award for Claire College Cambridge and was about to be called up – like everybody else . . . Then I got a letter saying would I like to do this [work at BP] . . .'.

Hugh Foss, Section Head at Bletchley Park.
(BPTA P431)

A reunion of Bletchley Park workers in 1987 (as guests of British Telecom, who occupied the site at the time), who had been recruited to the Newmanry and Testery sections forty-five years previously. Harry Fensome who worked on Colossus is far left. (Photo by Lionel Grech BPTA P94/14/1)

Despite this, the net still had to be spread more widely; and it was 'Oxbridge' that was baited first. Such angling made for an excellent catch, and even included some women: 'I graduated from Oxford with a degree in Maths (although my headmistress had told my parents that mathematics was not a very lady-like subject) and I was sent to BP for an interview . . .'.

The approaches by Oxbridge dons and deans were so successful that they were extended to other universities: Manchester, Sheffield, Aberdeen, Reading, and London. Interestingly, a number of female undergraduates went to BP simply because they did not want to be trapped in the few professions open to them then, like teaching:

'I was at the end of the first year of University Studies at Westfield College London, reading German with French. In 1942, it was ordained that women could not remain at University unless they undertook to teach . . . As I was at that time not prepared to teach I waited to see what kind of war work turned up.'

'After a year at Manchester University reading French with German, I decided that reading modern languages didn't make much sense so I left to join the

Forestry Corps. I happened to meet my old Headmistress and told her what I had done; she was horrified. A few days later (she must have had contact with the War Office) I had a telegram saying a railway warrant was in the post and to report for an interview in London.'

Like Topsy, the needs of Bletchley Park grew fast. The discreet quest for 'geese' had ever to be expanded. Now secretarial colleges were combed,[12] together with the Post Office, banks and even John Lewis shops:

'I learnt only at a recent reunion (2000) that I was recruited directly for the Foreign Office after my Secretarial course at St James' College. The college principal was asked for likely candidates. My name was obviously put forward because I suddenly got this application form from the FO and was simply thrilled.'

'I was working in a bank, and on the bank manager's recommendation I came here. I suppose they were looking for people with discretion.'

'I was working for John Lewis in Southsea. One of the Directors came down when I happened to be a Manageress. He learned that I'd got my call-up papers . . . [and asked] if I was willing to go to Bletchley.'

'I was with the Post Office Engineer Department at an outstation in Sussex. A friend – also at the PO – said he'd been offered a special place but had refused. Knowing I was qualified, he suggested me as a switch.'

Some of the Bletchley Park 'geese' seem simply to have happened on it. Ignorant of the machinations of recruiters, they 'somehow' or 'by chance' came to work at BP: 'I came to Bletchley by a stroke of luck. Before the war I was a secretary at the Bank for International Settlements at Basle in Switzerland. When war broke out I became secretary to British Military Attaché in Berne. [Then] I was called up as a RDF operator.[13] I was so bored and happened to tell a friend. He said "What a waste!" . . . and got me here.'

There were other BP workers who felt more like flotsam and jetsam, at the mercy of whatever fate summoned them. One soldier, for example, had battled in the defence of Norway, was interned in Sweden, then despatched to Northern Ireland where battalions were being mustered to go to Libya, only to be downgraded medically for home duties and sent to BP. Others, similarly, had to follow the vagaries of wartime:

'I worked for a Tea Company in St Dunstan's Hill where we were bombed so moved on to the Twinings Tea Company. When I started work at 16 in 1939 I was a junior shorthand typist. Then war broke out and all the men Tea Clearers were called up and eventually I became one. If you were in the food trade you couldn't leave during the war. Eventually when I was called up I got posted to Bletchley Park.'

'I did my training (as a Wren) at Tallyhewin Castle in Scotland for a fortnight and we had no idea what we were going to do. But in those days at 18 you didn't question. Adults asked you and you just answered. We were sitting in this room waiting to be interviewed for a "special category". We heard we would be up to our waists in water, underground, digging tunnels in the dark. We were so frightened that by the time we were all interviewed we all just said yes. We never did ask what is all this about.'

There were some recruits however who relished even the limited choice given them and who took as much control of their lives as they could. Interestingly, many of these were women: 'In 1943 I read that WRNS recruiting would stop on 31st December and as I had lost my boyfriend in the Merchant Navy, I always wanted to join the Wrens. So on 30th December, I went to Bristol with just enough money for my fare and walked all day trying to find out where I could join the WRNS . . . Finally I ended up at the far end of the Downs in Bristol, and the officer I met said she rather admired what I had done.'

Deference towards authority and its summons is not so prevalent in twenty-first-century Britain as it was sixty years ago. Now we are more likely to be 'invited' to an interview and there is an assumption of choice in our acceptance of a post or otherwise. Then, you simply followed instructions and passively accepted decisions made about you: 'I was considered old enough to serve my country and was accordingly summoned for an interview.' Despite inconveniences, your priority was to comply: 'The summons for the interview had been sent to my home address. I didn't actually receive it until the morning I was supposed to be there. I had just time to rush to the station and get the train.'

There was no question about your complete acquiescence in what was expected of you: 'Obviously one did not turn that kind of thing down – I duly appeared in the office above the car showrooms in Piccadilly for an interview during which my German was tested.'

The people who interviewed you similarly infused you with awe for their status and veneration for their superior talents. One such was 'the redoubtable A.D. Lindsay (afterwards Lord Lindsay of Birker and first Vice-Chancellor of the University of Keele) then Master of Balliol. I called at the Master's Lodge, a large Victorian pile rather sparsely furnished and which smelled strongly of tomcat.'

John Tiltman[14] features large in several recollections of interviews: 'Tiltman himself appeared to me almost the parody of a regular army officer with toothbrush moustache and rather clipped speech; as I was to discover later he was a man of outstanding skill and experience for whom I came to have the greatest respect.' One woman remembers him arrayed with several other BP chiefs before her when the ban on wives of BP employees was lifted: 'I sat in the middle of Travis' office on a hard chair facing Denniston, Josh Cooper, Travis and John Tiltman.'[15]

Another was 'interviewed by Frank Birch[16] . . . arrayed in muddy thigh boots and a terrible grey jersey with a large hole in it. He produced a document in Italian full of incomprehensible words like *sommergibile, incrociatore.* . . . He said, You'll soon pick up the technical jargon. When can you start?'

The formidable Miss Moore[17] is recalled by several: 'She was very "blue-stocking" . . . in her long black gown.' Others had characteristically varying experiences with their interviewers:

'I was taken by a porter down a long corridor lined with pictures. At the end, one of the pictures revealed a lift which took me up to a room where Mr Sanderson interviewed me. He was very good-looking, like the Duke of Kent . . .'

'An elderly, white-haired civilian greeted me in no friendly manner and told me his name was Pratt. He talked in a hectoring way about GCHQ, BP and Station X. All this meant nothing to me. It finally dawned on me that they must be one and the same place.'

'My interview took place in what looked like a railway carriage tucked away behind some bushes near Bletchley Station. It was conducted by two gentlemen – a retired Army colonel and a civilian who I learned later was a brilliant linguist speaking 16 languages fluently . . .'

Common to all the interviews are the references made to the secret nature of the work to be done, and the fundamental need for its concealment. Perhaps recruits were too young, too impressionable, too typical of mid-twentieth-century stratified society to question it. Indeed they would 'keep mum' not only for the period they were at BP, but for many years after, some for the rest of their lives. For example, one young women was engagingly (or patronisingly) asked if she 'could keep a secret': 'I answered that I really didn't know as I had never tried. . . . She said I would be considered for Special Duties X. . . . After being kitted out, 22 of us were drafted to the mysterious Station X. On arrival at Euston, we had no clues as to our journey, so we enquired from the engine driver where he was going. He replied with a broad grin and informed us that "the Wrens get out at Bletchley".'

The vetting process, like the interview summons, was unreservedly accepted by prospective recruits. There was no outraged remonstrance against the intrusion into one's private life, no Human Rights Act on which to call, no definition of civil liberties which one could, or would, cite. Neither were any preceding explanations – or even requests – made by recruiters to search into one's personal background: 'They seemed to know I was good at Maths . . .'. Nor were they ever challenged:

'I had to produce three references from various people saying whether I'd be suitable for something that was secret. . . . One of those was a friend of my

Wrens recruited from all over the British Isles. Featured are Elsie Merry (London), Margaret Reece (Cardiff), Olga Forshaw (Barrow-in-Furness), Kath Scott (London), Audrey Brickdale (London), Isabel Stewart (Aberdeen), Kath Eaton (Crewe), Phyl Turner (Nottingham), Val Jones (Swansea), Estelle Flett (Findochty), Katie King (Balham), Dorothy Perkins (Rushden), Barbara Marquiss (Leeds), Freda Tootal (Manchester), Helen Bone (Carlisle), Joyce Hewson, Kath Dunford, Pat Hanson and Rose Bull. (BPTA P352.09 – 27)

The gates of Bletchley Park, from the sale particulars, 1937. (BPTA P94.15.1)

father, an Admiral. He said, I don't know what your daughter is going to do but is it alright if I saw her bank statement?'

'For six weeks I was kept in limbo [at BP], quite free to move wherever I wanted, but no work – I was being vetted along with two other young women with me. Then we were all admitted to the Park . . .'

'In the intervening three weeks there were questions asked around my mother-in-law's place – by an insurance man . . .'

There was no question of BP recruits refusing the offer of a job when it came: 'I was in due course summoned to BP.' This was in spite of all the inconveniences suffered at interview: 'I was wearing my most untidy clothes and I hadn't had time to eat or drink, so I was in quite a bad temper when I got to the interview.' Nor were possible future inconveniences a deterrent: 'I was informed that I would be stationed within 50 miles of London and might be working underground in gum-boots. . . .'

But what was irresistible – and unquestionable – was being part of a secret so huge, so important that you could not even speak of it to your nearest and dearest. One husband and wife who met and worked at BP, but in separate work sections, tried to explain: 'It's absolutely true that because of the Official Secrets Act we were not allowed to discuss our work with each other, and we never did. I think the modern generation find that very hard to believe, but we didn't. Plenty of other things to discuss of course, but we had signed the Official Secrets Acts and that was it. We were conditioned not to speak. . . . It's a great pleasure now to be able to talk, not only to each other, but to others.'

Training for the new BP recruits entailed a hotch potch of courses. Perhaps BP's secrecy required itineraries that would confuse an interested enemy. Course venues were certainly diverse: 'first in London . . . then transferred to Bedford . . . then to Bletchley'. It was a similar case with trainees' use of time: 'I did a short course in Japanese, run intermittently – not every day – over six weeks.' So it was also with the trainees' use of their newly acquired skills:

'I went to school in Bletchley for a couple of weeks where I learnt to touch type. Straight from the school I went into the Enigma room . . .'

'I learned to type but it was quite a few weeks before I was introduced to "it" as I referred to my work in my diary.'

Of course, a more formulaic training was encountered in the Services, especially remembered by former Wrens:

'We were only at Northampton a fortnight where we were kitted out with our uniform and taught our left foot from our right foot and how to salute.'

'Basic training took place at Mill Hill London. The building, a partially completed hospital, stood on a windy rise. The early morning drill sessions in a small yard were taken by an elderly RN Petty Officer. We seldom saw him because of the fog, but obeyed the disembodied commands as best we could. . . . Within the building we had 'house' or 'galley' duties. We were issued with navy denim overall dresses which cleared up any remnants of vanity we may have cherished. I had 'house' which involved the daily scrubbing of four flights of stone steps, on hands and knees (nothing sissy like a mop) . . .'

'After being enrolled at New College Hampstead, we were lined up to have our heads searched for lice – a depressing start to my naval career . . . then a strenuous fortnight learning Naval etiquette, squad drill, domestic duties and marching up and down Finchley Road.'

After training, some Wrens were either 'told of a special job (they) could volunteer for' or were simply posted there, without explanation – an alarming experience for some:

'Six of us were put in an enclosed van and driven away.'

'After a fortnight the posting went up on the board. All the other Wrens were going to ports, but against my name was P5.[18] Being rather timid I was anxious to know why. The First Officer said I would be given a Travel Warrant to go to Euston Station and catch the 3.15 to Bletchley . . .'

Once chosen as 'special', trainee Wrens were given some unexpected extra preparations:

'We learned to fire-fight, and become first-aiders and a rescue squad. We were warned that if we were bombed we would have to look after ourselves. Our job was so secret, no-one would come to our rescue. So we had to be big brave girls from the start . . .'

Teleprinter course for WAAFs at Cranwell, near Grantham, 1941. Margaret Reid-Todd (seated front, first left) was posted to Bletchley Park soon afterwards. Colleagues inscribed farewell wishes on the photo such as 'Good hunting!', 'Through hardships to the stars!', 'May your future be brighter than Cranwell'. Among the signatories are 'Squibs' Newall, Gladys Turkington, Irene Phillips, Ann Ripley, Sylvia Sawyer, Iris Knowlson, Winifred E. Slater, A.B. Starling, Doreen Exton-Marsden, M. Brumell, I.R. Baird, I.R. Brown, I.M. Luke, S. Palmers, Dorothy Crandley, Shirley Savile, Felix Percival, Pam Higwell, Yvonne Lear and Rita Wood. (BPTA 43)

'We were all given a day's course in fire-fighting. They used one of the huts with duck-boards across it. We had to crawl over on our stomachs with a stirrup pump – the smoke created with burning oily rags – to find the fire. Funny thing is in films you see people coughing and coughing, but really you're like a vacuum cleaner, gasping for air.'

'For reasons I have never understood we were issued with sou'westers . . .'

Finchley Road in London, Talvera Camp in Northampton, Chippenham, Blackpool, Edinburgh, Compton Bassett, Scarborough and Wentworth Wood in Yorkshire ('horrible place it was then') – the BP training web stretched nationwide. One Wren remembered her training place with some remorse: 'Ten of us were posted to West Drayton to train on the operation of an Enigma machine, captured in Norway along with its Luftwaffe operator who was "minded" by an RAF policeman. To my shame and regret we taunted him, but he was the "enemy". Our shame was made worse when we heard he had left his wife and baby in Bremen . . . and knowing that Bremen was bombed hadn't any news of whether they were alive.'

In contrast, the reminiscence of one ATS woman is imbued with understandable pride: 'At Aldershot I did my driver training on the big three-ton lorries. We had to know all about the engine and change a wheel in three minutes flat – that was quite something. After a period of time I passed all that was required and then was posted to Bletchley Park – because I was a top driver and chosen because I was very good.'

Specialist training was 'hard going' for many, particularly Morse Code. It features in numerous recollections, [19] some of them amazingly detailed after sixty years' hiatus:

'I trained as a High Speed Telegraphist or Wireless Operator/Morse Slip Reader. I had never heard of a Morse Slip Reader but I will try and explain what the training entailed. The slip – or tape – would be carried automatically in front of the typist on a carriage . . . sent from other wireless stations. They were perforated tapes punched out on a machine looking exactly like a typewriter. The perforated tape would be fed into a machine named an Autohead and convert into Morse symbols that could be read by the receiver. There was no time to look down at the typewriter keys so we had to learn to touch-type. We also had to learn to read the Morse symbols on the slip which were a different shape to the old "dot – dash". To those of us who had never typed before this was all very new.'

But it was particularly hard having 'no idea at all of the finished product of my work'. Indeed, one woman, now a nonagenarian, comments of herself (though it could refer to the blind acceptance of their lot of thousands of BP geese): 'Fancy going to a job not knowing what it was! No wonder we were brainwashed!'

Assessment of these 'special' workers was essential. Following a training course at Rugby, the report by 'Special Intelligence' assessors revealed what they were seeking: 'This officer has ability and has understood the course well but has yet to learn the hard thinking and initiative needed to convert German intercepts into a "meld" of the quality Commanders expect.' Other comments included: 'Intelligent but not sound . . .'; 'Promising and steady . . .'; 'Good. Will reach commission standard . . .'; and 'She has widened her outlook by attending the course and should be able to do more specialised work on her return to BP . . .'.

The assessment of trainees about their courses and tutors, however, was often less than favourable: 'The training was a bit hit and miss. For example if you are breaking into something, you don't really have to know a lot of language. I hardly used the German I acquired. There was absolutely nothing mentioned about machine ciphers in the training.' Indeed, some BP workers stated: 'we didn't get any training; we were pitched right in . . .'. And some plaintive souls obviously felt they had missed out:

'There was no training as I was only checking the messages that had been decoded into English and typed into English and we had to check that the typists hadn't made any mistakes.'

'I wanted to be a driver but I couldn't drive.'

Whatever the experience, trainees were met with every ruse to keep the secret: 'I was told I was coming to BP on a Gas Course – poison gas that is – a subterfuge to retain the secrecy of the work being done at Bletchley.'

CHAPTER 3
First Impressions

'The military in shoes and ties . . .
Young ladies in summer dresses . . .
Men in open-necked shirts and flannels!'

'I was whisked away in the duty car way into the wilds – I didn't know then it was Buckinghamshire. . . . On arrival, I had to ask where I was!'

If you passed your interview for BP (and possibly completed training too), you would receive 'instructions from the Foreign Office' to depart from your nearest mainline station – perhaps Birmingham New Street or Edinburgh Caledonian – 'on such and such a date'. Then 'on arrival at Bletchley you will find a telephone kiosk. Ring this number and await instructions.' The 'cloak and dagger' approach

The interior of Bletchley station booking hall in the 1940s. (LA BS 36)

No. 1 platform at Bletchley station in the 1940s. (LA BS 40)

thrilled some, but terrified others: 'My poor father thought I was going to be dropped behind enemy lines.'

The journey to, and arrival in, Bletchley itself might not have been quite up to the promise of such adventure:

'I remember a dreary journey from Euston carrying a very heavy Revelation suitcase . . .'

'Bletchley station – a dreary place. . . . There were one or two others also making phone calls.'

However, if you were lucky, you were given more enthralling orders. You might have been given a sealed envelope (perhaps marked for your future boss, like 'Captain Andrews') with intriguing directions: 'Take the exit from the arrival platform, go to the station forecourt and report to a hut on the far right hand side marked RTO[20] and show him but DO NOT GIVE him your envelope. He will direct you . . .'. Sure enough, your RTO man would seem to be sufficiently privy to your mission to give you further instructions: 'Go down the station approach, until you come to the main road, turn right and in a few hundred yards you will come to a country lane, go up that country lane until you come to the iron gates. There will be two or three sentries there. Approach one of them, show him the envelope and he will direct you to Captain Andrews.' If you had been conversant with uniform protocol – as this source was – you might have been surprised, like

The approach to Bletchley station, c. 1937. (LA BS 85)

him, to find that the 'sentries' were in fact 'blue–hatted guards with revolvers, not sentries with fixed bayonets. This denoted a top–secret establishment.'

Other new BP recruits had a rather less auspicious arrival. One, a member of the ATS, was told to report to Bletchley Park one Christmas Eve:

'I got to Bletchley some time round about midnight, got off the train. Everything was in darkness, but there were some iron steps going over the bridge. So I went up there and that led me to a gate which I pushed open. There wasn't a soul about. I walked through and had no idea where I was of course, but there was this big house in front of me. Nobody about so I walked up to this big house, carrying my kit bag up the steps into the door. Everything was deadly quiet then somebody came into view and said, What the hell are you doing here? So I produced my [letter]. Christ! he said. You are not supposed to be here. Anyway they contacted Hut 3 somehow. [When I went there] they took one look at me and said, Oh God we'd better send you home until after Christmas! I finished up on my parents' doorstep next morning . . . I was called back in a day or so.'

It took some 'pluck' then (in the idiom of the day) for a young woman to arrive alone in a strange town, in the middle of the night, during wartime, in the black-out – and in an era when women were not expected to hike around unescorted. After all this, there were still unexpected challenges to face, like from the company they might find themselves in:

'I was surprised to be met by an army sergeant with a small utility bus. He examined my pass and told me to climb aboard. About 10 other girls joined me, including one called Doris who sat down beside me and continued to chatter all the way to Bletchley Park. When we reached the gates it was apparent that the place was heavily guarded by more army personnel. On seeing this Doris became very excited exclaiming "Goodee! The army are here – we'll have some fun!" At the time I was a shy young lady, very anti men and I made a mental note to lose Doris at the earliest possible moment.'

'I must have arrived rather late and walked up a path way from the local station. Two young women were asked to show me the way to the Canteen for a meal . . . I remember we had soup and a massive plate of stodgy milk pudding. My two escorts spoke not a word to me but I learnt quite a bit about their private lives in their conversation with each other.'

The worst realisation for some was that they were at journey's end: 'In the early hours of the morning I was decanted onto Bletchley station, and met by an army captain. He took me home where his wife gave me breakfast . . . I asked when we were going on. He looked blank and asked, Going on where? I said, Oxford or Cambridge. I couldn't believe it when he said we weren't going anywhere, that I'd arrived. Bletchley is now absorbed in Milton Keynes but then it was a railway junction surrounded by brick-works with no redeeming features, and populated entirely by railway workers or men who worked in the brick-works. I might as well have found myself in outer Mongolia . . .'.

Now that they had arrived, the new recruits' cardinal duty was to be sworn to secrecy. They were 'ushered' or 'escorted' into 'some office' in the main house. They were told about the nature of the work, its extreme importance to the war effort and the fact that it was covered by the Official Secrets Act. Then everyone had to sign a form agreeing that they would not divulge anything to a living soul, being warned of dire consequences if they did. Even imprisonment was mentioned: 'We were told in no uncertain terms that this was a very important thing and we would go to the Tower if we breathed a word.'

The west front of Bletchley Park mansion seen from St Mary's church tower, c. 1900. (BPTA P97.14)

The 'mansion' at Bletchley Park, described by most BP workers as 'the main house', is depicted in various ways: 'BP was awe-inspiring – the guards on the gates, the drive up to the great house, the grounds full of huts and large concrete blocks.' Its black–and–white timber–framed aspect, however, fooled no one. First impressions were of 'a large/very grand/sprawling/ghastly/hideous/grotesque . . . Georgian/Victorian/mock-Tudor/early 20th century redbrick mansion', or, quite simply, 'this big and rather ugly old country house'. The house itself had 'shiny wooden walls and rather ornate mock-Tudor staircases' and 'no carpets in my day . . .'. There was 'a small dining room on the right as you enter; teleprinter rooms to the left of the main staircase; and upstairs included a Home Guard office'.

Agreed by all to be large, the house stood in grounds described, according to the chronology of development: 'with a huddle of huts'; 'with several large huts'; 'surrounded by an assortment of huts and outbuildings'; 'with Nissan huts in all directions'; 'full of huts and large concrete blocks'. Many also recall 'a boating lake, a tennis court and numerous trees and bushes'. For one, the memory of the flora is tinged with some poignancy: 'I remember two magnolia trees in the Park, which are still here and very much more mature . . .'.

However, there was a sharp reminder of the clandestine nature of the work to be undertaken: 'the entire perimeter was surrounded by a security fence of upright metal laths, bent over at the top and surmounted by several layers of barbed wire . . .'.

More extraordinary though were the lengths to which those in charge at BP went in order to maintain secrecy. One resident of the cottages described her first experience of the mansion: 'I was taken into a room in the Big House where there was a long table covered in a grey Army blanket. At the table sat several senior officers one of whom read me the Official Secrets Act. They then told me I was the youngest person at that time to sign. I was thirteen.'

For the many new recruits who arrived in the dark, BP in daylight revealed to them an unforgettable sight – not the buildings or grounds, but the people: 'It was a village confined on the grounds . . .'. There were 'countless people . . . passing in and out of the Main Gate, strolling, talking, and sitting around. There was a great seething of people – always movement – comings and goings. The whole thing reminded me of a bustling London railway terminus.'

The other wonder was that they were 'nearly all in civilian clothes, but there were also many in Navy, Army, and Air Force uniforms . . . service personnel mingling with civilians!'

It was a genuine shock for these 1940s recruits issuing from a stratified society to see not only the mixture of personnel, but also their 'seemingly casual' dress. One put it down to her ignorance of contemporary British fashion: 'Coming from Paris, I didn't know that baggy trousers and unpressed tweed jackets were worn by wandering young men who were probably the boffins of the place. I did note they seemed to be rather respected . . .'.

However, it is clear that the casual approaches adopted at BP extended beyond one's attire: 'One of the first things I heard when finishing a late shift in the dark was a group of naval men frolicking in the lake nude with shrieks and giggles.

An outdoor rehearsal group for the Bletchley Park Drama Group, 1945 – 'Combined Ops'. (BPTA P94.36)

Apparently this happened quite often, and the gorgeous officers – some very blonde – were homosexual.'

One officer recalled the chaos that was lunchtime – civilians and service personnel all eating and chatting together: 'My most vivid memory is . . . threading our way through a kaleidoscope of chattering, moving people to collect our food when a young girl, moving towards us and looking the other way, deposited an entire plateful of macaroni cheese down the front of the Chief-Commander's best uniform.'

Dazed by the magnitude of the place and perplexed, no doubt, by the unfamiliarity of what seemed normal, new 'geese' had little time to acclimatise themselves. It was off to work at the earliest opportunity: 'I was met at the station by an army coach and when I got here, put into a wooden hut [where there] were rows and rows of machines and two women in charge. We had to leave our bags on the coach and were given a card on how to work this machine. We were then taken over to C Block and met the man in charge . . .'.

CHAPTER 4
Where the 'Geese' Worked

'X is the name of our perishing station
The board at the gate gives you no indication
Of what we are up to, for all that it states
Is "Go very slowly through our secret gates".'

In the early days, before huts proliferated like measles, Station X's secret work was carried on in the main house – all a mystery to one woman who was a member of the (very small) administrative staff at the time: 'I worked for MI6 in the tower – the only room I worked in while I was here. My boss was Eddie

Hastings.[21] There was a team of six people and we worked in shifts round the clock. It was the unofficial tea-room, all very hush-hush and run by the boys. They used to go in the little room next door at the top of the stairs, but of course we didn't know what was going on, it was all very secret.' This sense of imposed – and accepted – ignorance was to become the mainstay of BP's existence.

The earliest work huts to accommodate the influx of 'geese' at Bletchley Park were solid and quite small. The first and 'best built one' was constructed out of Canadian pine and was about double the size of a large lounge – 40ft × 16ft (12m × 5m). The domestic analogy ends here however, for not much comfort was intended. Flexibility was of an essence: internal partitions needed to

Workmen constructing BP huts, c. 1940.
(BPTA P204.005)

One of the BP carpenters at work. (BPTA P94.22.5)

Construction of a BP hut roof. (BPTA P94.22.9)

be put up and pulled down as required – sometimes when incumbents were still working there: 'The rooms were always changing shape as someone called Commander Mackenzie (who had once been a stage scenery expert) was always shifting the partitions about. Once I was typing and suddenly his saw came through the partition I was facing and narrowly missed my head . . .'.

These first huts were put up quickly: 'It wasn't a rush putting up the huts, it was a panic.' Bob Watson, a carpenter and joiner who worked in the Park for forty-five years, was in the original team building the huts – along with subcontracted local coffin makers. He described the huts taking shape 'as if coming off an automated assembly line . . . The contractors whacked them up. We all went behind them sealing and lining them out, then Hubert[22] came round with whoever was going to be in charge of the hut, and marked out a partition – how many rooms do you want and what size? Right, marked on the floor, so no getting away from it – that's where it went. Then all the coffin makers went berserk putting partitions up and bashing on – you could get them up in one weekend with 20 or 30 people . . .'.

Nobody knows precisely how many different buildings were constructed between 1939 and 1945 – perhaps as many as fifty, several being built and demolished in BP's lifetime. For it was not an orderly development. Many had their functions changed several times over the years. For example Hut 1, built on the site of four 300-year-old elms next to the main house, began life as a base for 'the wireless people' with trial Morse intercept positions installed. Later it became a Transport office and included in its seven-year existence a sick bay, lavatories and a fire-fighting trailer and pump house. No wonder then that some reminiscences include the admission 'I'm not sure where I worked . . .'.

Nevertheless, some huts acquired certain distinguishing features in the maze confronting new recruits. One, for example, had a main corridor nearly a third of a mile long. The most famous huts – numbers 3, 4, 6 and 8 – later emerged in history as the 'key code-breaking huts', although only those who worked in them then had any inkling about their importance. Memories of Hut 3 are particularly numerous:

'It was only in Hut 3 that I understood what BP was all about. Life thereafter was quite exciting at times, at others sad, when colleagues went missing on secret missions.'

'On New Year's Eve 1944, I caught the eye of a Wing-Commander from Hut 3[23] and he came into our office to invite me to have a glass of champagne in their Watch, the Holy of Holies! Much to the amusement of my co-workers I went. He showed me a great horseshoe-shaped desk with telephones that filled this large office, and the special phone that went directly to Mr Churchill's under-ground offices in Whitehall. This was the heart of Hut 3 Watch . . . a real thrill to see.'

The abiding memory of people throughout BP – whatever their hut or room number – was the complete isolation of its workers from others:

'We of course never communicated or ever spoke to anybody from another room about work. Though I do remember some dashing about passages when *Graf Spee* and another [ship] were sunk. But that was none of my business. Anyway to me they were just "big boats".'

'We didn't go into any of the other huts; that was something we didn't do. There was no need to. We never discussed our work, even with the people we worked with while outside.'

'Our Watch' from Hut 3, c. 1944: Wg Cdr Oscar Oeser is third from left, front row. This photo is courtesy of LACW Kent, who is second from left, next to him. (BPTA P279.014)

As ever more instant buildings were needed to accommodate the flocks of new 'geese' arriving, so the design became ever more utilitarian – and massive. Buildings of 30,000 sq ft were planned (thirty times the size of a semi-detached house); Canadian pine was abandoned for plasterboard and asbestos; and remnants of the Leons' old Bletchley Park disappeared forever: 'Hut 10 was built on the site of the old maze; when we moved in, bushes from the old maze were still stacked outside – some fool set fire to them.'

Soon, a new building phase – of concrete and steel construction – came into operation. Strengthened accommodation was essential for the new machines – one of them an alarmingly named computing mechanism called the 'Bombe':[24] 'Some of us had a tour of the building that housed the computers – called "Bombes" by us. They looked like 6ft high switchboards pierced by thousands of wires.'

The first Bombe machine (one of five in the hut) was installed in Hut 11 in August 1940. By mid-1942, there were 220 Wrens working in the hut over every 24-hour period – between 70–80 women on each shift. 'The Bombes never stopped working and if, on a very good day all the main codes had been broken there was always a backlog of unbroken codes from previous days.'

However, other specialist huts were needed for ever more complex instruments: 'We had punch equipment, sorters, a couple of dozen re-producers, multipliers, tabulators, banks of printers, ten or twelve collators . . .'. Hut 14 was

An internal corridor in one of BP's blocks. (BPTA P94.24.11)

the 'Traffic and Cypher office: a teleprinter room for 120 machines [containing] all the telegraph circuits, and an adjacent telecoms room with audio amplifiers, multi-channel voice frequency, and the main distribution frame.'

The construction of such huts led to a new concept, for the housing of even more vast machines tended by even more 'geese' – two-storey concrete blocks, numbered A to H. For example: 'Block A housed Hut 10 from mid 1942. Hut 10A's Air Section was re-housed here too. The Air Section from the 1st floor of the mansion and the Naval Section (from the ground floor) also moved in . . .'.

The sections servicing BP's secret needs demonstrated the versatility needed by an organisation that was outgrowing itself almost daily. Among these huts were those for Chauffeurs, the Home Guard, the Engineers' Workshop, Stores & Goods-in and Rest Rooms: 'The next hut down was the women in khaki, the FANYS[25] – all the vehicle drivers – they virtually drove anything in the procession to and from work.' One specialist building, the Telephone Exchange, built in 1941, is a poignant reminder both of BP's air of resilience and of its transience: 'It had five large console desks in it and was constantly manned day and night. It had 18-inch reinforced blast-proof walls with a 12-inch blast-proof roof. When it was broken up in the early 1990s it took them a month to remove it.' Another had a more gentle retirement: 'One of the huts was sold to Bob Watson's father for £20 and removed to his garden.'

When BP workers have returned to visit Bletchley Park after perhaps fifty years, they are amazed by their ignorance of the place, only now dispelled:

'Large sections of the Park were off-limits to us, so walking into the Mansion [today] was something I had never imagine . . .'

'There was so much I never knew about the place in which I had spent three years. We were cocooned in our own particular section. The amazing thing was we were handling messages from all over the world, day and night, year in year out and never knew the context of them.'

CHAPTER 5

What the 'Geese' Did

'No mention whatsoever may be made either in conversation or correspondence regarding the nature of your work. It is expressly forbidden to bring cameras etc within the precincts of Bletchley Park including Elmers.'[26] (Official Secrets Act)

After being surreptitiously recruited, enigmatically interviewed, secretly trained and sworn to secrecy, there was another reminder awaiting BP workers: 'All newly-arrived personnel will attend a Security Talk in Room 18, Main Building on the Sunday morning after arrival at BP at 10.00 hrs.' Then they were deemed ready for their work assignments – to the exclusion of all others: 'What all those people did I've no idea . . .'.

A rare picture of BP workers in operation during the war. (BPTA P284.001)

New workers would be confronted by a wide variety of machines and gadgets: 'There was so much of the work done on machines; moderate machine ciphers[27] had been in use for years, commercially that is.'

Although typists used conventional pre-war long-carriage typewriters, there were odd requirements: 'I registered the messages – lots of them – typing on large size paper about 18 inches × 24 inches long in order of receipt . . .'.

The 'Type X' machine was thought to be a mechanical forerunner of computers soon to be developed at BP. Working at it was also a novel experience: 'It rattled and clacked through the night . . .'; 'It was like an old-fashioned mincing machine with an end bit with little cogs on.'

And it was busy: 'There was about 30 of us in the room at any time typing messages. We had a drum officer and we would drop the drums in and work them round with a pen . . .'.

For so many of its staff, BP work was incomprehensible. They were perplexed by the 'Undulator . . . producing sticky tape which I had to stick up for the telegram message – miles of the stuff', and the 'Flora-Dora' . . . a terrific machine and really antiquated. You had a wheel in cardboard with different sections . . .'. It was like a weird, Kafkaesque[28] dreamworld:

'In the front there were some civilian women, doing things at a desk without any machines. So if they took it from us or gave it to us, I just don't know, we didn't ask.'

'Everything at BP was in code of course, and we had no idea what we were handling.'

Along with Kafka, Aldous Huxley might well have found some material for his *Brave New World*[29] in BP's ethos of 'not knowing': 'We kept very much to our own groups, chiefly from the security angle. I always thought it better not to know . . .'.

'E Block Auto Room' seems to epitomise early BP gadgetry. One reminiscence paints a particularly evocative picture:

'You saw benches situated at right angles to the central walkway, solidly built and quite long, loaded with equipment – typewriters, perforating machines, autoheads, Morse keys and other paraphernalia. On a board above the bench was a row of pegs where tapes hung, wound into a figure of eight, waiting to be transmitted or typed. Each bench had the name of the place that particular operator was in contact with. Exotic names to me then such as Melbourne, New Delhi, Alexandria, Suez, Port Said, Malta, Cairo, Calcutta, Colombo, Toronto. There were clocks on the wall showing the different time zones in these parts of the world.'

The Bombes, huge deciphering machines designed by Alan Turing to crack the Germans' Enigma code-settings, were the precursor to the famous 'Colossus' computer: 'Everything about the [Bombe] machines was played down – very low

The Signal Office at the War Office in London, showing the desks for Italy, Melbourne, Cairo – and 'Station X', c. 1941. (BPTA P421.001)

profile, no big deal. I always thought the secrecy side of it was wonderful considering all the people who knew about it. No one spoke anything about it for years and years after the war.' The following amalgam of verbatim descriptions, mostly from Wrens, evokes what it was like to work these 'noisy and cumbersome' machines:

'The Bombes were bronze-coloured cabinets about 8 ft tall and 7 ft wide. The front housed rows of coloured circular drums – the naval colours were dark blue, black and silver . . .

The 'brainy people' would say, 'We think it could be something like this', and would send the Menu . . . [which] contained a complicated drawing of letters and numbers. This told us how to plug in the great red pigtails of plaited wires . . .

The back of the machine defies description – a mass of dangling plugs . . . and a multitude of wires, every one of which had to be meticulously adjusted with tweezers to make sure the electric circuits did not 'short'.

The drums also had to be put in a certain order . . . [and] were put on the machines with clips which were quite stiff – we got sore fingers unclipping them.

Then you'd switch on and the machine would keep spinning and spinning . . . until it came to what was called a 'stop'.

Giant Bombes connected together at BP. (BPTA P364.4)

As each run was completed, one row of drums was taken off, replaced by another set. During the next run, all the newly removed drums had to be inspected and trimmed. Their circles of copper wire brushes were set at an angle and if a single rogue wire bent and caused a short circuit, that run was invalid – and repeated.

If the drums stopped *suddenly*, it signalled that the code-breaker had stumbled upon the right combination. The three indicator drums on the right would be noted down – hopefully that would be the answer.

Immediately the Controller was informed – another anxious wait before being told "Job up, strip down!" – then you knew the cribs[30] were correct.'

In October 1944 the Bombes were averaging 35,000 hours of operation per week and helped decode nearly half the daily average of 4,500 intercepted messages. As for why these monsters were so noisily operating, their minders had but the vaguest notion – which they would never divulge anyway: 'I never heard the word 'Enigma', because we were not allowed to discuss our work off duty. We were all very conscientious about this and the secrets were kept throughout the Park.'

A celebrated feature of BP machines and gadgetry was their complex communicating system of pipes and tubes:[31] 'The teleprinter messages – marked

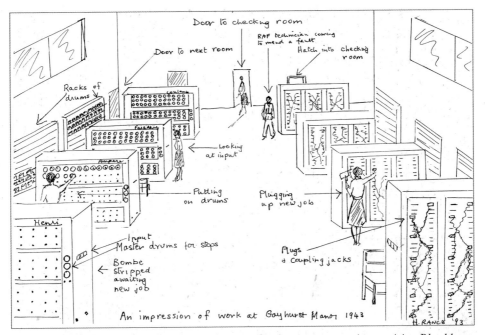

Sketch by Helen Rance of the Bombe machines at Gayhurst, an outstation servicing Bletchley Park, 1943. (BPTA 36)

Message conveyor system at Bletchley Park. (BPTA P94.24.1)

"Top Secret", "Urgent", "Immediate", etc – rocketed through the vacuum system landing with a hiss and a bump.

Earlier attempts involved less sophisticated gadgets. One woman remembers the "Heath Robinson" . . . named after the cartoonist who drew fantastic machines . . . This was an endless chain with clothes-peg clips to carry the messages . . . . But we kept losing messages, so "Titch" had to go and pick up the lost copies, bring them back to the security man.'

Earlier still, BP carpenter, Bob Watson had constructed the legendary wooden connecting tunnel between Huts 3 and 6: 'There had to be some brown lino on the bottom for the office tray to slide on. [First] we had a broom handle and banged it. Then it was a hook and some string with a big knob on the end, and you'd thump the box through . . .'.

There was a constant maintenance programme for the more complex machinery. At the forefront were engineers from BT,[32] around 400 of them in C Block alone. Their careful routine inspections limited the emergencies:

'We had a book of instructions like a school exercise book.'

'We would work virtually for 24 hours making up the new wiring forms and inserting them into the drums of Type X machines. I think we did it in very good time, in spite of blinking, tired eyes.'

'Maintenance was done on a regular basis rather than waiting for something to go wrong. If you do your maintenance properly you have reasonable control.'

The legendary wooden tunnel – or external ducting – for the message conveyor system between huts. (BPTA P94.24.7)

Thought to be part of BP's Engineers Workshop, with rotors lined up for maintenance (BPTA P409)

BP worker waiting at message receiving point. (BPTA P94.24.3)

Despite all the machinery, there was a lot of pencil and paperwork: 'I wish I had a clearer memory of those everlasting slips of flimsy paper . . .'. The Bletchley Park Trust Archive still has some wartime pencils used by the 'geese'.[33] It was 'pretty tedious' to work by hand before machines could decode enemy messages: 'trying to break the code in a roundabout way. We worked on huge graph paper from the top left-hand corner using figures, adding them together. If we reached a certain collection of numbers at the bottom, we'd broken it.'

One worker remembers 'distinctly' foolscap sheets with violet ink. Uncharacteristically for BP, he speculated a little: 'Who compiled these, I wonder? They often started off with "Source saw a document . . ." It was disguised as if it came from the Resistance. (Apparently it was the Watch wrote these – and they went to Churchill). I would be the only one on night shifts and have the leisure time in the night, getting a file of these and just reading them through, out of interest.'

In order to process enemy messages each unit of people had a specific, often repetitive, task to complete, like a self-contained link in an unknown chain. They only knew they had to do the task, pass the material on to the next and repeat the task – a human conveyor belt: 'We went in and sat at the table next to the hatch and gave out these messages as they came along and sent them back to the typists.'

However, some could share in the interest that their work aroused in others: 'Our job was to list the messages with the time and the number of words. The people from Hut 3 were always coming in, looking at your list for a particular time they thought might help them. Six [o'clock] would be the weather. When they were expecting anything, that would be really exciting, because they would come in more often and look at all the messages. It was always busy.'

An important instrument in organising the mass of data in the early days was the Hollerith punch-card machine:[34] 'At the back of the building were ramps where lorries came in regularly with hundreds and hundreds of cartons of punched cards ready to be processed.' But the system did have some setbacks: 'We would poke a steel pin through the cards to make sure they had been sorted correctly. . . . Occasionally we would have a tear-up – one card had bent and put all the others out.' And despite being aware that this was somehow crucial to the war effort, workers 'didn't know what it was, to be truthful. . . . Somehow it decoded the message and then it was put through the large machines in the next room.'

However, there were some perquisites to being in the Hollerith section: 'It was wonderful as members of staff actually found out that their brothers or husbands or fathers or boyfriends were still alive because they found their names on these sheets detailing who had escaped from a prison camp in Germany. They would state the uniforms worn, the regiment of the chap who had escaped and if they had a knapsack or any supplies. The messages were obviously sent out for the Germans to trace them.'

Other paper-organising aids were quite homely: 'We had a big table with

Cartoon of 'BP filing' by D. Hukton. (From BPTA 21)

thousands of brown cardboard shoe-boxes full of index cards . . .'. This indexing was extremely detailed and comprehensive, with individual 'geese' being given a specific focus: 'I had to keep a card index of the name of every Italian officer and other rank mentioned in any signal as well as any info about him. We were also supplied with cuttings from Italian newspapers, and given interminable lists of men in the Italian Air Force who had been decorated – the Italians handed out decorations like Smarties . . .'.

Cartoon of breaking the code (writing at desk) by D. Hukton. (From BPTA 21)

It was a most effective system. A visiting high-ranking American was nevertheless bemused: 'Goddamn, if this were the Pentagon, there would be rows and rows of shiny filing cabinets with nothing in them and you do it all in Goddamn shoe-boxes!' Perhaps he would have been even more bemused to have witnessed another of BP's organisational routines: 'We had to sort the dustbins out in case anyone had put confidential paperwork in there. We all had to do it.'

Collected, listed, sorted and indexed, the paperwork had also, somehow, to be analysed and translated to make sense. It was the compilation of vast, complex – and interlinking – jigsaws to break the code. The function of one particular room, the Fusion Room, was to 'co-ordinate the information from reading the logs with information from the decodes. [We took] these sources and fed it out in two directions – for interception to go on or for decoding.'

The log-readers themselves had a coordinating role: 'Weather reports would sometimes contain important clues. Coupled with direction finding you could build up a complete picture of what was going on in a particular [German] unit . . .'. Some 'coordination' involved a little creative thinking: 'I was dealing with broken messages [with] great gaps in them, damaged in transmission. We had to think up what to put in the middle of them.'

Specialist translators were essential to 'building up the picture', but 'the job of translating captured German documents was painstaking and slow. Subjects were highly technical – [about] welding on a submarine, or specifications for flying bombs – and one spent hours reading English text books to see if one's translations made any sense. There were also endless instructions on the procedure and organisation in the dockyards – the translation was intended to make it easier for the Allies to make use of the dockyards as soon as they were captured.' However you could not be allowed to compromise security: 'I wasn't allowed to translate more than three or four words. One wasn't, because again this secrecy . . .'.

The seemingly most glamorous, and usually the most celebrated, of all the jobs at Bletchley Park was of course the actual code-breaking, although newcomers were faced with a treadmill of routine: 'The job of decoding required a lot of slog, application and a certain amount of imagination . . .'. Nevertheless, many ex-'decodists' also indicate the sense of absorption that kept them working non-stop for hours: 'When anyone started a task, there was no way he could be persuaded to pass it over to someone else. It was their job to get it done as far as possible. I was hooked on decoding . . .'.

DESIGNATED RESPONSIBILITIES

In January 1945, the number of people working at BP had doubled[35] in just two years. They were divided into thirty-three different sections, the largest being 'the Bombe section in Hut 11A and local WRNS outstations'[36] having quarter of the workforce (2,106).

The smallest was the 'Interception Co-ordination Section' where one of the two personnel was the 'pigeon man', Charles Stuart Skevington: 'I can remember the great patience of the pigeon man waiting for the birds to go in the loft so he could remove the message cylinder.'

Born in 1906, Charles Skevington started his interest in pigeons in his native village of Milton Bryant. When he married, he worked for the Newport Pagnell corn millers. A Special Constable at the outbreak of war, he was asked if he would fly pigeons from Bletchley Park. His son remembers him 'driving a bus from Newport to BP' to tend the pigeons kept in the loft above the BP garages. His carrying case carried a single pigeon at a time and was used by agents flying out to France and Germany and parachuting in: 'Once, a pigeon was partially crushed on landing, but still made it back to BP. Another, shot by Germans through the crop again still made it home to BP. Father cleaned the wound and treated it with iodine. The bird subsequently recovered and flew several more missions . . .'.

The view over the stable-yard, ice-house, engineer's house and glass-houses, with huts beyond, c. 1940s. (BPTA P94.22.7)

The device used for attaching messages to the pigeons' legs was 'kept in Mother's button-box. It was in three parts – a clip that went round the bird's leg, a small plastic tube which clipped onto it, and a screw cap which had a fork incorporated in it. The message was written on a very small piece of tissue paper and put into the fork. He rolled up the whole thing, inserted it into the tube and screwed the cap on. On the pigeon's return to the loft, Father removed the message and handed it on to the necessary people . . .'.

Unlike the majority of BP workers, Charles Skevington was given some token of appreciation for his sterling work: 'He owned a silver pen in recognition of owning the fastest bird in the services.'

Nearly 10 per cent of the workforce in 1945 were in 'Administration', including 152 house staff (cleaners, handymen and watchmen), 151 maintenance workers, and 139 catering staff. There were 29 people working on billeting;[37] 14 medical staff, and 20 staff worked in the Registry and Despatch Office. Finances were looked after by 15 members of staff, and a further 8 dealt with staff records and recruitment. BP defence was overseen by 5 ARP[38] wardens; the workers' NAAFI[39] was run by 4 people and their Recreation Club by 3; and there were 5 barbers.

The largest support service was the Transport Section – 169 personnel in 1945. The records of the week of 14 January 1945 show that 79 men drivers and 50 women drivers carried a total of 3,210 passengers. They travelled 25,000 miles on passenger runs, 1,400 miles on despatch runs, and 5,600 miles on 'special journeys'. The latter included vehicle collection, 'furniture removals for HQ', 800 London van runs and 570 luggage runs. They used a fleet of 137 vehicles based at BP including 42 'Utility' vehicles, 40 coaches, 30 saloons and 23 vans: 'We drove Ford V8s, shooting brakes, and there was a Wolsey and a Hillman. . . . We would wait in the lounge for the phone calls. Whoever was there answered and then you could find yourself going down Watling Street to St Albans with despatches or to the Admiralty. If you had just come back and someone else was sitting there they would take the next job.'

Also unique to BP was the Police and Security section, 44-strong and quite separate from the armed soldiers on sentry duty:

SNOOPER!

Cartoon of guard on patrol by D. Hukton. (From BPTA 21)

'We [the Military Police (MPs)] were in uniform manning the gates and the perimeter. Every vehicle that arrived was stopped, all passes were checked and any suspicious ones were directed to the office for the MOD [Ministry of Defence] people to deal with. Nobody, but nobody got through the gates without a properly recognised pass – including all the drivers who we knew personally. We weren't armed, just the normal police equipment – truncheons. We would wear a blue covering to our caps – different to the normal Redcaps who were outside on duties relevant to the armed forces – and a triangular blue flash on the jacket sleeve with "VP" on it. They created that Corps for all "Vulnerable Points" which they thought were subject to sabotage or whatever.'

MPs undertook their duties zealously. When one young woman was between billets and had her luggage in the hostel, she was 'challenged by the MPs on the gate. Anyone not conforming to the usual shift times was suspect. I was put in the guardroom while he rang my shift boss – she had to come down and rescue me.'

The MPs were also 'part and parcel of the internal fire brigade' – whose routines included working 'two Coventry Climax pumps. When the weather was nice and warm our practice consisted of one pump near the lake and a booster pump halfway. So we would water the lawn in front of the house!'

Those in charge of a section had primarily to ensure there was utmost secrecy throughout their section at all times. The following circular reveals a constant underlying anxiety: 'Commanding Officers of those lower commands which are authorised to receive ULTRA[40] information are to be instructed that such messages are for them only and are to be destroyed by fire immediately action has been taken on them. No exception to this rule is permissible . . . [If lower commands receive them] the information must be translated into, and transmitted to them in the form of, operational orders, so worded that if captured or intercepted by the enemy they could not be traced back to ULTRA information alone.'

The private communications of staff were also closely monitored: 'emergency telegrams' and 'out-of-normal-hours private telephone calls' needed special permission from your Head of Section.

Moreover, section leaders had an awesome duty to ensure that the special functions of BP operated as smoothly as a leviathan with innumerable tentacles could. There is an intriguing glimpse of Head-of-Section workings in a memo sent round by 'AD'[41] on 31 March 1942:

'Will Heads of Section please report how many of their staff are working the 2-shift system, i.e.
1 week – 9–4
next week – 4–midnight
Whether this is being done from the necessity of the work; the lack of space; or for the convenience of the workers?
Are these workers taking 1 hour or half an hour for meals?'

There is a revealing answer to this memo from one of the heads, Alan Turing. who replied by return, seemingly uneasy with the implication that colleagues were exploiting the system:

'There are four of our staff who work –
    one week   9–4
    "   "   9–6
    2   weeks   4–12

This is done owing to shortage of space.
They would otherwise work 10–6 always.
They *naturally*[42] take 1 hour for meals.'

'BP geese' generally had a strong sense of duty to do whatever job was needed – to be adaptable: 'Sometimes I did work of others who were away, or helped in the shift-officer's partitioned-off room where there was a piano-type machine. . . . We had to know how to do each other's job.'

The biggest individual responsibility – keeping the secret – was largely self-regulated. Although all had signed the Official Secrets Act and were living in an era of respecting 'authority', it is remarkable how completely the secret was kept. The 'geese' tried to explain why they didn't cackle. For example, a generous salary was attractive: 'I was paid between £25 and £30 a month – staggering and a lot of money . . . they told us we were getting this much to keep our mouths shut – they actually told us that.' However a pittance could be equally successful: 'I feel our pay was too little to attract "baddies". . .'.

Many point to a heavy-handed indoctrination – being 'brainwashed' and 'too imbued to think about' divulging the secret:

'Everyone in wartime was very security conscious and at BP the emphasis on security was heavy and unremitting.'

BP workroom with hatches, blackout curtains and message conveyor system. (BPTA P94.24.8)

'It still seems very strange to be talking openly about what went on at Bletchley Park.'

'Secrecy was so ingrained in me that for 30 years I didn't even tell my husband. If he asked what I did in the war, I just said it was something to do with radio and changed the subject.'

Others believe that the key factor was simply the persistent culture of dutiful discretion in the 'strange life we led. . . . You simply did not talk shop, never, never.' Others again suggest that it was patriotic fervour that kept 'geese' gagged: 'Our work was tedious and continuous but we kept going knowing that the war would end one day.'

Even today, some 'geese' cannot bring themselves to utter a sound: 'I can recall so much about my time at BP but having signed the Official Secrets Act, most of it must still be regarded as classified.' These view anyone who divulged anything as a traitor: 'I'm disgusted and appalled that people can betray their own country and consequently their own conscience. We were dedicated and so should they have been.'

Money, patriotism, the expectation of your seniors or of your peers – it is a moot point as to which of these motives, if any, would be as powerful today. Perhaps it sufficed once simply to regard any indiscretion as 'treason', a crime punishable by death. Now, it is more likely that participants would need to understand and appreciate the whole operation – be actively involved and be committed to the cause – before their silence could be assumed.

CHAPTER 6

Working Conditions

'It was hot, noisy and very bewildering . . .
I don't think any of us worked so hard in our lives.'

On 27 March 1941, a visiting dignitary[43] visited Bletchley Park. He arrived at 11.30 a.m., met Commander Travis, and was given a typewritten 'idiot's guide' to the normal working day of Hut 3. He met 'the Administrative Officer, Major Edgar. He is in charge. His duty is to ensure the smooth running of Hut 3 . . . everything except the intelligence side of the work.' The visitor would have nodded acknowledgement to each of the unnamed 'geese' busying themselves before him: 'Each watch consists of a Duty Officer; No. 1; a Military Advisor; an Air Force Advisor; and 4–5 members.'

Then the Hut's work process would have been patiently explained to him, for he needed to be another person leaving 'Station X' not just impressed with an efficiently run organisation but convinced also that its work was indispensable.[44] Future finances and development were at stake.

However some felt they had limited usefulness when VIPs came: 'We were very young and we weren't told things – we were only juniors. On the day Winston Churchill was coming, I was told to make sure everything was clean – get rid of the milk bottles.'

'V is the visitor – distinguished brass hats
Come snooping around to see what we're at.
We sweep the place clean with dustpan and
    broom
And move all the empties to some other
    room.'[45]

HRH Princess Royal on a visit to an outstation listening to Morse code through headphones, with Major Haigh explaining, April 1944. (From Joan Brown, née Stevenson BPTA 22)

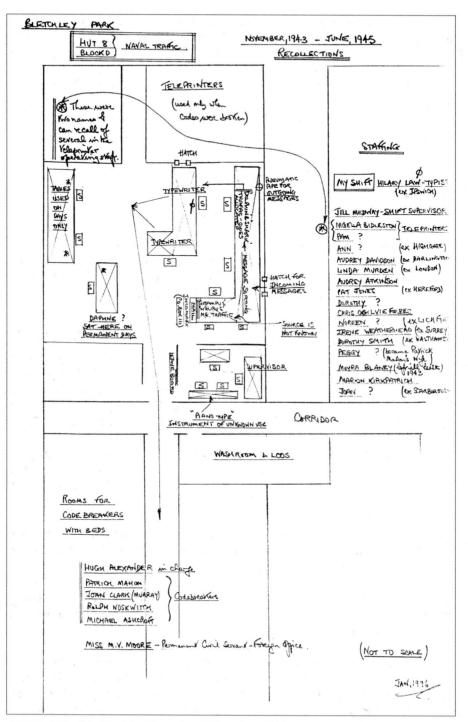

Sketch of Hut 8 in Block D, November 1943 – June 1945, as remembered in 1996 by Hilary Powell née Law. (BPTA)

The 'notes to assist all new arrivals at War Site'[46] were a taste of 'normal' working life ahead: 'CONFIDENTIAL: not to be left lying about!' What followed included information on billets, meals, laundry, shoe repairs, doctors, ration cards, transport and the recreational club – hardly revelations that would lose Britain the war, but it underlined the ethos of absolute secrecy Other security procedures reinforced the message: 'From behind the huts there was a cinder path that was one of the guard walks. You never saw them go back or down at the same time.'

Instructions on correspondence were particularly forceful:

'When writing to aliens anywhere or people overseas, including Eire and N. Ireland, the following Box address will be used, and on no account will Bletchley or surrounding district be referred to by name:
C/o Box 222, SWDC
Howick Place, London, SW1
All correspondence written from the above address will be posted in the special box provided in the Hall, Main Building (marked "Letters to be posted in London"). On no account will they be posted elsewhere.'

Shift work was the norm at BP: 9 a.m. to 4 p.m; 4 p.m. to midnight; midnight to 9 a.m. Each lasted a working week which was six days long: 'A lot of us worked 12 days and then had a weekend off to go home.' For some, the evening shift was 'by far the most unpleasant. The early part seemed almost as full of people as during the day while one's free morning was useless for any social purpose. One ended the shift at midnight tired and irritable but unable to sleep.' For others, the night shift was 'very tedious . . . Since most of the traffic was intercepted during the day there was not a lot for the night shift to do.'

Views, though, differed on this: 'The night shift was the best, the most productive. The day had more people about – distracting discussions were apt to take place. But at night one could work away quietly with nothing to disturb concentration.' But sometimes shifts merged or were abandoned altogether:

'After being on duty all day we would be fetched out of our beds. The message was, Will you come? We can't manage. So as quickly as possible we got togged up again and off we sailed forth to another night's hectic work.'

'At the time of the Battle of Alamein I had one half-day off in 9 months. I frequently worked late into the evening and slept on a camp bed in the office as it was too late to drive home . . .'

As for graded posts, BP had as hierarchical a structure – despite its ethos of open-necked shirts and Christian names – as any other organisation of contemporary Britain. Women filled the lower grades: messengers, 'compilers' and 'card-indexers' remained on the bottom rung as 'Grade III Temporary Assistants'. The lowest wages of all were for fifteen-year-old female school-leavers – 13s 6d per week (about 20 per cent of the national average):[47] 'I was

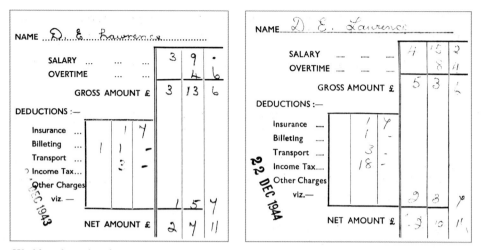

Weekly salary slips for a BP worker 1943–4. Despite her 40 per cent salary increase over the year, her take-home pay increased by just 25 per cent – owing to heavier income tax. (BPTA)

introduced to BP by my mother who was already employed as a waitress there. She got me an interview with Miss Stevens who was in charge of the messenger girl service in the Park. I started work the next day. I was 14½ years old.' Temporary typists started at £1 3s 6d (40 per cent of the average). Academic qualifications might earn a woman extra, but she could still spend 'all the days typing', for this was what women were expected to do.

BP's administration situated in Room 10 of Hut 9 epitomised 1940s-style bureaucracy, run by a man supervising women. Captain Seabrooke, the Senior Officer, was assisted by Miss Maine (billeting); Miss Good (birth certificates); Miss Appleton (National Savings – you could buy 6d and 2/6d savings stamps); Miss Warner (visitors' lunches – 1s 6d); and Miss Forder (fines for late payment of meals). Room 10 issued BP passes and collected a fine of 2/6d for losing them – nearly a quarter of a hapless school-leaver's weekly pay.

One notice posted up outside the room illustrates the wonderfully implausible expectation of administrators – that information will be assiduously heeded. Memo 'AD (A) no. 42 of 8th May' stated: 'the following AD (A) Memos are hereby cancelled: No. 1 of 10th March 1942; No. 2 of 12th March 1942; No. 17 of 7th April 1942; No. 21 of 14th April 1942 and No. 37 of 27th April 1942.'

Notwithstanding, the occasional irregularity was a powerful reminder of BP's unremitting obligation to keep its secrets: 'I remember John Harrington, because he disappeared. When I went into the Accounts Office I had the shock of my life. There were these two burly MI5 men either side of him. He was such a clever man and I'd asked Miss Molesworth why someone so clever was doing this sort of job. But he seemed to know a lot about everything so I told Miss Molesworth and that's how he was picked up – he was a spy.'

The working environment itself came as a shock: 'We lived in a sea of mud, traversed by duckboards, and everything seemed cold, damp and foggy.' 'I worked in most of the blocks' said one worker, 'always moving because the number of people was increasing.' Others though had a less extensive horizon: 'The only room I ever saw in all the two years I spent there was the one we worked in – Hut 7. . .'.

The most common recollection is of a working environment that was at best utilitarian and at worst comfortless:

'Tables covered in army blankets . . . top furnished with ashtray, eyebrow tweezers and note pad . . . a folding wooden chair . . .'

'Concrete floors. . . . The cleaners came in about 6am. There was a rush to go to breakfast at 7am as the whole room was a fog of dust which settled on your papers so they always felt gritty.'

'The toilets with floors all wet and horrible.'

'Even now when I smell ionization I am again in that hot, low-ceilinged room in the early hours of the morning, watching the machine in a haze of cigarette smoke and trying to keep my eyes open through the interminable runs, half-mesmerised by the slow rhythmic clicking as the drums crept round on the spindles. In those days to sleep on watch was a greater crime than murder. We sat with our checkers, talking and smoking to keep ourselves awake. The end of each run signalled a short burst of frantic activity changing drums then back to

Sketch by D. Hukton of the EVT Gen Room at Bletchley Park. (BPTA 21)

smoking and talking. There was very little we didn't know about each other on that job.'

The facilities for heating were pretty basic: there were pot stoves in the huts, but it was the huge computing machines that provided some unplanned supplementary heat – and prompted workers to call their working environment the 'Hell Hole': 'We worked in our shirtsleeves, although our guide today said we worked in our underwear – I don't think we did!'

'Stifling in summer', the huts were 'unbelievably cold' in winter: 'For weeks one looked out at the icicles outside hanging from the eaves. I bought a pair of Morlands' lined boots in Oxford for £3 and felt guilty about my extravagance for days . . . and wore nothing else for weeks. (The boots lasted 25 years!)'

As for lighting, you could be forgiven for believing your work was subterranean:

'We worked in concrete blocks that had all the daylight blacked out permanently, so we had to have compulsory sun-ray treatment.'

'The windows were covered in mesh so nobody could look in and only the top fanlight opened. We worked day and night under flickering neon lighting.'

Water supplies were another challenging feature of working life at BP; there was either too much – 'Hut 4 would flood. We put a pump under the floor. It used to run every morning for perhaps half an hour . . .' – or there was too little – 'Hut 7's water supply was cut off by a lorry working on Block D construction which crushed its water main.'

The physical demands were unremitting: Wrens had to be 5ft 8in tall to reach the top of the plug board of a Bombe machine: 'It was tough and tiring. We worked in pairs, at top speed, one plugging the back, the other slinging dozens of metal "drums" on to spindles at the front.'

The noise too was 'terrible', 'deafening':

'. . . as the drums revolved each row at a different speed. So there wasn't much talking during the 8-hour spell.'

'No-one heard one enter the room.'

'We couldn't hear the air-raids of doodlebugs . . .'

'It was like working in a factory', said one worker, for dirt and grease were inherent in the BP work routine. One memo entitled 'Secret Cipher Orders No 4: March 23rd 1942: Type "X" Drums, Care of . . .' included the instructions: 'The drums will be thoroughly cleaned daily. . . . A thin film of oil or Vaseline will be applied to the flush contact surface after every four hours' working. In no circumstances will drums be put into operation with the flush surface dry.' It was impossible simply to keep clean and tidy:

'Watchkeepers came on duty in correct uniform, gleaming white shirt, stiff collar, jacket buttoned. By the end of the eight hours, white shirts were covered in black grease from the drums, fingernails broken, thumbs and forefingers bruised from squeezing the heavy clips fastening drums to spindles.'

'The table I worked at every day – without fail I knocked into the corner so much that the skirt I habitually wore was quite distressed as if a cat had been deliberately stropping on it.'

'We had to join this tape and put blue-dye on it wherever we joined it. This dye would get on your hands and be a job to get off.'

Perhaps even more gruelling than the physical work were the 'very dull and monotonous tasks' or slack periods with 'little traffic'. 'We would take an

Sketch of colleagues from Section V in A Block by M. Cornwall-Jones – 'We were a very congenial set of people in this section.' Her key to the 'exhibits' is as follows: Exhibit A: S/Lt R.R. Howard-Williams – the Führer. Exhibit B: Mr W.T. Ewing, Deputy Führer. Rather poor likeness; Willy is tall and thin! Exhibit C: P/O P. Goatly, WRNS. The hair is remarkably like, but Prue is rather larger altogether. Exhibit D: P/O B.M. Godman, WRNS. A very good likeness of Mary at work. Exhibit E: Miss A.L. Dent. Jill's hair is not really so neat. Exhibit F: L/W J. Tackaberry WRCNS. Another good likeness. Exhibit G: S/Lt P.H. Vennis. Note: red hair & freckles, also younger than drawn. Not a good likeness of Philip except for the cigarette-holder. Exhibit H: Miss M. Cornwall-Jones. The best likeness of the lot! Exhibit I: The Führer's thinking-cap. Exhibit J: Hirohito's death mask, carved from a puff-ball. Exhibit K: Ditto, carved from a stale bun.' (BPTA 14)

uncomfortable kip on the hard tables . . .', but for those who could not take such rest 'life at Bletchley seemed to drone on and on'.

Moreover, precision and total accuracy were deemed crucial – and it all weighed heavily on BP workers: 'A lot of concentration was needed and speed was continually impressed upon us – thousands of lives could be saved. This constantly hung over one's head, which made for a great deal of pressure. . . . There was no room for slipshod work.'

It was frustrating therefore if your attempts at '100% accuracy' were thwarted by machine problems:

'If your Bombe stopped quickly, your heart sank as it probably meant a wrong stop.'

'The machines were always breaking down.'

Further, the sense of isolation that permeated BP even during the day worsened at night: 'The registry was very lonely on one's own at night away from others. The rest of the Block was empty at night. Most eerie.'

Overriding all these pressures of course was the constant imposition of silence surrounding all work topics: 'People find it amazing that we didn't talk about our work. I didn't even know what my boyfriend did when he was stationed at Bletchley. Occasionally you might get a sniff of something important happening. An excited look on the face of a superior officer would be a tell-tale sign. But on the whole everything was hushed up.'

PROBLEMS

'We often received shocks plugging up the gate at the back of the Bombes, but the technicians had more – they had to put their hands into the entrails and crashed about all over the place.'

With so much electrical current surging through BP's huge machines, there were inevitably accidents. One technician was shocked to the core: 'A Wren operator was prettying herself using a metal mirror which slid across two large electrical terminals. There was a bright flash, the mirror evaporated and her lipstick shot across her throat. I was working nearby. The scream made me look up. I thought she had cut her throat!'

He also witnessed a fire in the Machine Room (MR): 'A glue was created from a black concoction of Benzine which was stored in glass Winchester jars on storage racks in the workshop adjacent to the MR. One was knocked off the shelf – it broke, and the contents seeped under the workshop door. There was a flash – the Pitchmastic floor caught fire and black smoke filled the MR. We had to use fire extinguishers because the local fire brigade had difficulty getting past gate security people.'

The Blitz left BP largely unscathed; there was the occasional bomb alert, prompting the order 'Steel helmets and under the tables!' but only one explosion, early in the war: 'A bomb landed in the spinney and the blast moved Hut 4 on its foundations. It slid and stopped when it met the wall of the telephone exchange on the other side. It didn't even break a pane of glass. The lads got some big railway-type jacks and a couple of sleepers and just eased it back in position.'

Indeed, BP's crises were generally because of the nature of its work and environment: 'The equipment was so heavy the floors collapsed.'

The frenetic nature of BP work is a common theme in reminiscences: 'Hectic evening! Worked against time but made it . . . Place in uproar.' One diarist in early 1944 took care not to reveal any details: 'Sun 25th April: Shift 4–12pm. Hectic day at work . . . Upheaval – new arrangement – table to ourselves – OK!' Later, in June 1944, she has, uncharacteristically, no entries for three days, then:

'Sat 6th June: We invade France – all seems well. Days off cancelled. Work's just a shambles!. . .
Sun 11th June: Shift 9.00am–8.30pm. Busy – very
Mon 12th Started the nightmare
Tues 13th Gosh what a day! Refused to stay late
Wed 14th Hectic day!
Thurs 15th Another hectic day. Got rid of "nightmare"!'

An enduring problem – insufficient personnel – was outlined in a letter to the Government from Heads of Section including Alan Turing:

'21st October 1941
We are intercepting quite a considerable proportion of wireless traffic in the Middle East. . . . Owing to shortage of trained typists however, and the fatigue of our present decoding staff, we cannot get all this traffic decoded. This has been the state of affairs since May. Yet all that we need to put matters right is about 20 trained typists.
    . . . In July we were promised that . . . sufficient WRNS would be provided (for Bombe testing). It is now late October and nothing has been done. We cannot help feeling that with a Service matter . . . it should have been possible to detail a body of WRNS for this purpose, if sufficient urgent instructions had been sent to the right quarters.'

Almost by return, Prime Minister Churchill arranged for the requisite staff to be sent to Bletchley Park.

The unrelenting pressure of security, however, was sometimes the most frustrating to endure. One engineer described the over-zealous attitude of one of his colleagues: 'One hot summer night I was called to Hut 3 to attend to a malfunctioning teleprinter feeding material direct to the Cabinet War Room in Whitehall and was duly admitted by a Wren officer after checking my lapel badge pass. Because of the heat, I took off my dust-coat, located the fault but needed a replacement part, so I told the Wren I needed to return to Hut 14 and she let me out. Five minutes later I returned, but she refused me entry because I did not have my lapel badge on.' The hapless engineer pointed to the badge on his coat

Hut 3 and Hut 6. (From Mrs Marie Bennett BPTA 275.001)

hanging on the chair, but she still refused saying it was 'more than she dare do'. Finally he had to borrow a badge from a colleague and was later reprimanded for breaching security regulations.

One of the worst times for BP was when, in addition to variations of settings on Enigma machines, the German 'constants' in their secret messages also changed daily. These were the frequencies and 'call-signs'[48] providing a dependable base for building up a translation of the rest of the coded signal. Then the German Navy inserted a fourth rotor[49] to complicate the Enigma code still further:

'It was imperative the messages were read before sinking any more of our shipping. Sometimes a lone lighthouse keeper could provide the clue by forgetting to change the code, but it was very depressing when perhaps three days had passed without reading German codes.'

'We couldn't break a thing – a very frustrating time for us.'

A reassuring internal memo written by Stuart Milner-Barry, explains what he calls 'the self-regulating process' of code-breaking: 'As long as the keys come out easily everything goes swimmingly, but as soon as things become more difficult the production of menus outruns the capacity of the Bombes to absorb them. . . . If the process goes on long enough the ideas of the cryptographers become exhausted. . . . But the arrears are gradually worked off and presently equilibrium is restored and the cycle starts again. . . . The fact that stringency never seems to last for any length of time must indicate that there is some fundamental self-regulating process in operation.'

But failure there was, and BP workers felt it keenly: 'One very bad occasion was when Convoy PQ17, largely of merchant ships with escorts, was sailing round the North Cape into the White Sea. But the *Tirpitz* and the *Scharnhorst* got loose, and unfortunately our decoding efforts were not timely enough. . . . There was a great slaughter of these ships.'

One crisis point – D–Day – involved an unexpected grounding: 'We started at midnight and the Head of the Watch said, "Before you young ladies sit down tonight, I want you to come and have a look at this map." He showed how all round the south coast the Army, Navy, and Air Force were grouped ready for invasion the next morning. He said, "Because of that you will not be allowed to speak to anyone outside of the room tonight or go on your canteen break." I didn't think about it much then, but I've thought since – how did they think three Wrens in the middle of Bletchley were going to warn Hitler we were about to invade?'

REWARDS

There were compensations for all the difficulties – the War bonus, night–shift payments, the Special Operator bonus and overtime. But for many, the only bonus was the actual pay-day itself: 'This was a Parade (in camp) everyone welcomed. An NCO called our names and we had to reply with the last three digits of our official number . . . with a salute to the officer in charge, the sum of 2/- a day was given into our left hand.'

And of course, to go on leave and escape the hurly-burly of BP was keenly anticipated: 'HQ was very kind and allowed me a few weeks to spend with my husband when on leave.'

However, feeling involved in breaking the codes was one of the greatest incentives of work at BP:

'It was interesting when everybody knew there was something going on, they would be in and out. . . . We never saw the translated version of the messages. They would tell us what was going on though, as we were part of breaking the code. They were very good at telling us.'

'It was a great thrill when you knew your machine had the winning hit.'

Nevertheless, not many 'geese' have this recollection: 'We didn't know that the Enigma cipher was being broken – or how valuable this was going to be. Reading the logs we knew all about the messages but they were put on a separate sheet. We used to speculate about this for a long time . . .'.

Eventually the policy of 'knowing what you need to know' was stretched to include these once peripheral log-readers: 'One day, one of the civilian mathematicians from Cambridge, told us what was happening. It was realised that there was so much checking on the logs that we ought to know what was going on.'

Notwithstanding, some loyal 'geese' who were not 'in the know' continued to marvel at the obvious import of their work: 'We all had an enormous sense of doing something worthwhile at BP.' The 'decoders' themselves naturally derived enormous enjoyment from their personal achievements: 'No work that I have ever done in my life has been more fascinating or given me greater satisfaction.' But even those who hauled machine drums around could share that sense of fulfilment: 'Life was rough and tough but I loved my work.'

Obviously, the most gratifying 'bonus' was when the hard work paid off and there was cause for celebration:

'When all their heads were down slaving away, if someone shouted 'Clear!' all the room cheered! . . . Once the codes were broken it was all hell let loose.'

'It was very exciting sometimes when we had seen a message about the convoys and a day or two later we learned that they had been attacked by the RAF – we really felt that what we were doing was having some effect on the war.'

One woman had reason to savour her particular success:

'In early 1943, I was on duty on the night shift alone. We were going through a sticky period; the Italian codes were making no sense. I decided to have one more go . . . suddenly a message began to appear. I shouted for Leonard Hooper in the next room and he rushed in and I told him the message was making sense. He literally seized my paper, shouted, You've done it! You've broken it! and tore out of the room and down the passage to Josh Cooper. There was great excitement that night, for the message was that the Italian airforce was preparing to leave North Africa. The news was radioed to the British RAF in Egypt and subsequently night fighters shot down almost all the Italian transport planes carrying troops to Sicily and Sardinia. For this breakthrough in decoding, I was summoned to Josh Cooper's room and congratulated. I will never forget the thrill of it!'

For many 'geese', the most enduring reward while working at BP was in the forging of relationships there:

Some members of the German Night Fighter section of Bletchley Park, c. 1944. Standing, left to right: Pat Smith, Edith Davidson, Janet Smith, Florence Brooke, Vincent Chapman. Seated, left to right: Molly Blakeley, Catherine Payne, Brenda Gough. In front, left to right: Joy Parker, Jeanne Phillips. (Courtesy J.V. Chapman BPTA P94.12)

'Several marriages took place or were agreed upon while I was there and liaisons flourished . . .'

'BP contained a network of longstanding relationships. . . . The Section [would] ensure that arrangements for shift-working took due account of them, for if one was working three shifts, it was difficult to do much "carrying on" with someone on a different shift. Then if a relationship had broken up, it might have been advisable to reshuffle the shifts. On the whole the system worked pretty well.'

Such 'carryings on' succeeded despite the best efforts of zealous security guards. One reported how he had assiduously kept watch on three consecutive mornings to observe 'a young married woman leaving the Park, coming off night duty, dressed as if she had left a Turkish Harem . . .!'

However, partners were excluded from BP workings. An RAF Flight engineer on the Sunderland Flying Boats commented that his wife had been 'a WAAF Corporal stationed at BP working on decoding. We did some of our courting in Bletchley. On leave, Kay would book B&B at Railway Cottages near the station. We married in 1946. Only then did she say that she knew of my destinations to the Far East from coded messages long before I did.'

Another woman wrote: 'I didn't meet my husband until after the War. He didn't know what I'd been working on during the War. We never really discussed it. He knew I had Christmas cards from people I worked with.'

Some partnerships seem to have been prejudged for their suitability: 'Before they revealed the Enigma secret to the logreaders, they weeded out quite a few and sent them overseas. Corporal Parlow sat opposite me and he had married a Czech woman in Bletchley. . . . He was sent to Cairo.'

And there was a sinister impression of being hostage to the knowledge that you had: 'I had the feeling that once you had been to Bletchley and knew Enigma was being broken, you didn't leave. . . .'

One ATS officer was shocked by her discovery:

The Orderly Room Sergeant brought me a large envelope, thicker than usual, marked SECRET. . . . "The DR[50] just brought this, Ma'am," she said, "and it was marked urgent." I opened it and inside there was another envelope marked TOP SECRET. This was serious stuff – no-one but the Chief Commander or me was authorized to deal with it. . . . It concerned one of our ATS sergeants who had lately married another sergeant working at the Park. The authorities were concerned that she might constitute a security risk. I opened the dossier and began to read, my eyes nearly dropping out of my head. I simply couldn't credit the extraneous detail of this girl's life that was contained in the dossier – concerning her parents, her extended family and even her friends. It sticks in my mind that her grandmother had once had an affair with a Turk! I knew we had all been security vetted [but] it was not a comfortable feeling, speculating how much the Secret Service knew about my life.'

CHAPTER 7
Boffins and Debs

'I is Intelligence, the boys in the Park
They all need a haircut but please keep it dark
The question I hope to be answered one day
Is how can a corpse look intelligent, pray?'

THE BOFFINS

The best brains in the country worked in BP's 'rarefied atmosphere'. Most 'geese' saw themselves as 'minnows' alongside the 'Boffins' who 'could do the Times crossword without writing in a single clue. They could visualise the answers in their head.' Conscripts from the Pioneer Corps, who built tennis courts for BP workers (reportedly on Churchill's instructions), must have been bemused to see these Boffins emerging from night shift 'looking anxious and exhausted. They wore a strange assortment of ancient overcoats, old macs tied with string, woolly hats made from tea cosies and sometimes pyjama trousers showing underneath everyday clothes.'

Sketch by D. Hukton: 'Intelligence speaking'. (BPTA 21)

Among the Boffins recalled as 'incredible characters' were: Hugh Alexander,[51] 'the British chess champion who wrote the chess articles in the Sunday Observer and Daily Telegraph . . . a very thoughtful man – on a visit to the USA he brought us back nylons and lipsticks . . .'; John Herival,[52] who 'would go to [his] digs close to the Park and after supper would sit in front of the fire in [his] landlady's house and think . . .'; and Rush,[53] who 'had a fascination with maps. There was a map reference for Tito[54] with a scrappy message saying, "Attack!" Rush checked it in his slow methodical way and it was Tito's HQ. Tito was moved out before the attack because of that.)

Of course, what the BP 'minnow-geese' loved about their Boffins was their eccentricity. The Boffins' legendary absent-mindedness – or their deliberately odd behaviour – compensated for their awesome brainpower. It gave mere mortals a sort of responsibility of care over them – or at least an interesting performance to watch.

Dr Barfield 'wandered around in a dream – he often got lost. He had to be rescued occasionally when he was wandering off down the road, muttering to himself . . .'.

Jack Good[55] 'was a hypochondriac – he seemed to be popping pills all the day, but he was very healthy and very energetic.'

Max Newman[56] 'dressed in his old fawn burberry[57] and carrying a dead hare by its hind legs, was pacing up and down Bletchley platform searching for something. I asked him if I could help. He had lost his ticket. We failed to find it and I assured him that he was so well known, they would believe him. No that was not his worry. Until he found it, he could not remember if he was going to Oxford or Cambridge . . .'.

Michael Trumm 'could sit thinking about a problem without moving for an hour and then come out with his conclusions. When he smoked, the cigarette was put into his mouth, he would remain stationary and no ash would come off until it began to burn his lip.'

Neil Webster[58] 'was walking down a long corridor with a pencil in his hand, and he ran the pencil all along the wall – there was someone standing in a doorway and Neil just ran the pencil right over them, quite oblivious to them.'

Leonard Hooper[59] 'was volatile, emotional, brilliant, unpredictable. Something of an undisciplined rebel but intensely professional and hardworking.'

Stuart Milner-Barry's[60] memorial service at Westminster Abbey in June 1995 described him as 'so unusually distinguished a man', remembered not only for having 'significantly shortened the Battle of the Atlantic' with his decoding work, but also for 'the battered but treasured attaché case, the long blue overcoat and the office-going hat . . . the woollen muffler and the woolly gloves.' Another reminiscence concerning him was tinted with a rather less rosy imprint: 'I went home after my wife gave birth because the child hadn't lived. Milner-Barry rang me and said, Don't worry Bob, stay away as long as you like. I can understand your difficulties. Well, I thought, that was very generous of him, but when I received my pay-packet at the end of the month, I'd been docked for all the time I'd spent at home.'

Several 'geese', unabashed with their name-droppings, were understandably thrilled at having worked so closely with great minds:

'Peter Benenson, the founder of Amnesty International, worked in the same hut as me.'

'I worked with Henry Read, the poet who wrote the fine poem "The Naming of Parts".'

'A.J. Elm the writer was known here as Mr Landboat.'

'I remember Peter Calvocoressi as a 30-year-old officer with masses of black curly hair. When I saw him on TV he was in his eighties with masses of white hair . . .'

However, certain Boffins created unwanted pressure for colleagues: 'Freddy Edwards would put quite searching questions and wanted you to look very closely at your material to see if anything matched his information and then he would disappear again . . .'; 'Freddy Greenwood would suddenly appear to make sure everyone was doing what they were supposed to. He looked just like Conrad Veidt – drawn face, monocle, very Germanic looking.'

Indeed, some 'geese' felt threatened by what they saw as an 'invasive habit of frequent visits'. One Boffin 'was not one of our favourite chaps. He was self-important and dull. He became an eminent professor of history, an esteemed historical author and a knight. And he was our *bête-noire*.'

Others inspired much affection and respect:

'Professor Hugh Last,[61] a dear man . . .'

'I had a great affection for Shaun Wiley[62] because I'd come back from a party and was sick, I'd had too much to drink. He got down on his hands and knees and cleared it all up . . .'

'Mr Harry Hinsley[63] was the nicest, most approachable and friendly person you could ever have met. I was about 17. When you are that age and people around you are so callow they didn't want to talk to you, it was wonderful.'

In a contemporary note to his section from Frank Birch written on 25 May 1945, the esteem felt for Harry Hinsley was clearly apparent: 'Harry Hinsley has left (Naval) section. That sentence hardly makes sense. The body has already lost limbs and functions; with the collapse of Germany it is losing more. But Harry was a component of our bloodstream. His loss will be felt by all of us, from the head throughout all the members.' Frank Birch[64] himself is recalled with some relish: 'His private passion was that of Widow Twankey in the annual pantomime.'

Boffins' leisure pursuits are also fondly remembered:

A rare photograph of Harry Hinsley (right) with Jocelyn Bostok (left) and Elspeth Ogilvy-Weddeburn, and Charles Morris, son of Christopher and Helen Morris in his pram, c. 1943. (BPTA P94.3)

'Asa Briggs[65] in the Sergeants' Mess – playing ping-pong and getting absolutely red in the face and leaping about.'

'Mr Smith, a very elegant and large man who danced beautifully.'

'James Robertson, Director of the Sadlers Wells Opera Company – organised concerts and opera rehearsals. His deputy was Stephen Usherwood an author of children's books.'

Some Boffins had an added advantage:

'"Duggie"[66] was a tutor – young blond and incredibly handsome . . . I still have vivid memories working under him . . .'

'Bryn Newton-John,[67] a handsome devil who occasionally invited one to dance at our evening socials. He later became father of Olivia[68] . . . He was a good singer.'

'We thought all the Americans had walked out of Hollywood especially Telford Taylor[69] – he was an absolute dream to look at and he was so nice. If he said Good morning, you just melted at the knees – he was absolutely lovely.'

One BP worker remembers 'a group of very smart Americans' arriving in the summer of 1943 under Captain William P. Bundy who later became 'very active in the Kennedy administration. . . . They were an interesting lot – businessmen, mathematicians, admen, chess players of course. . . . Alfred Friendly became editor of the Washington Post, Langdon van Norden the chairman of the Metropolitan Opera Association, Lewis Powell a Supreme Court Justice, and Bill Lutwiniak created cross-word puzzles for the Washington Post Magazine. . . . One became a prosecutor at Nuremburg.'

Three Boffins feature prominently in BP reminiscences. Their composite portraits drawn by 'geese' are inevitably arbitrary and incomplete, but offer perhaps fresh perspectives on legendary characters.

Josh Cooper[70]

'It was a privilege working for such a man – a brilliant cryptographer and brilliantly absent-minded.'

'A sweet, shambling academic with a photographic memory, capable of incredible hunches . . .'

'A wonderful coiner of phrases – he had been "belunched" if whoever he was trying to contact had gone to lunch. . . . He said he should be called "Netma"[71] – Nobody Ever Tells Me Anything. . . . He had three trays – "In", "Out" and "LBW" – Let the Buggers Wait.'

'Tall and burly with a large head topped by unruly black hair which he had a regular habit of pulling back from his eyes, fronted by heavy-lensed dark framed spectacles – the model of an absent minded academic. . . . He came over to give us a lecture. He'd be walking up and down and then start scratching his head, gradually working his way backwards until he was scratching his back like a contortionist.'

'He was noted for his absent-mindedness. He left BP clutching his hat in his hand and holding his briefcase on his head . . .'

'Sometimes he would be drinking a cup of tea by the lake looking rather puzzled, then suddenly he would look up with obvious relief and throw his cup into the lake! He would come to work in his pyjama top.'

'Josh always managed to keep his cool – people appreciated his sense of humour.'

Michael Cooper, Josh's son, was only four years old when the family moved into the last house on Wilton Avenue just before the Park gates: 'I don't remember much of my father – he wasn't there very much. [He] worked all the time. We were usually in bed by the time he got home. He would sleep in on Sunday. We would see him for lunch, listen to ITMA, but then he would cram his hat on and head for work again. . . . He knew all the time that people were putting their lives on the line. . . . He was a modest man. After the war all he would say was that he believed he'd saved some lives and that was what he was proud of.'

Angus Wilson

In the preface of Penguin's reprinted 1958 edition of *Anglo–Saxon Attitudes* (considered to be Angus Wilson's masterpiece) the biographical note has no specific reference to his crucial role at Bletchley Park: '. . . born in the south of England in 1913 . . . childhood spent in South Africa . . . educated at Westminster School and Oxford . . . joined the staff of the British Museum Library in 1937. When the War came he helped towards the safe storage of the British Museum treasures before serving the rest of the War in Naval Intelligence. . . . While trying to emerge from a period of depression and near-breakdown, he began to write short stories in 1946 . . .'.

Some BP memoirs include what might have been the seeds of this 'near-breakdown', including the antagonism of 1940s society towards homosexuals:

'Angus Johnstone Wilson was thin and highly strung. He spoke in a high, squeaky and immensely affected voice. . . . He lived with and was totally dependent on a male friend called Bentley Bridgwater with whom he would periodically have screaming fights followed by nervous breakdowns . . .'

'We christened him "John–Willie" and his boyfriend Muriel. He had very long hair which was unusual for men at that time . . .'

A group photo of Section 5, c. 1943, with Angus Johnstone-Wilson in the front. Other names known are (back row) Clifford Smith (first left), M. Cornwell-Jones (fourth left), Graham Sumner (4th right), Jo Kirk, (3rd right), Philip Vennis (2nd right), Prue Goatly; middle row: John Statham (1st left), Willie Ewing (2nd left); front row: Rona Ross (2nd left), Isobel Sandison (5th right), S/Lt Howard Williams (4th right), Mary Godman 2nd right. (BPTA)

Though Sylvia like all her swains I do commend,
and on "Sweet Sue" I hourly do depend;
Though to make Gwen my Guinevere I do intend,
and Joan like Joan of Arc to worship to the end.
It's oh! to be gay
with Kay.

Angus.

Photo of Kay Pickett née Harrison for whom Angus Johnstone-Wilson penned the poem 'Oh to be gay with Kay'. (BPTA)

'Angus Wilson was my first conscious encounter with a "queer" and I found him simply repulsive. He used to mince into the room, swaggering, and wore what were outrageous clothes in those days – a bright yellow waistcoat, red bow tie and blue corduroy trousers. His nails were bitten down to the quick, he chain-smoked and he had a horrible cracked sort of maniacal laugh! Anyway he was extremely clever.'

Later considered to be 'undoubtedly one of the three or four major figures to have emerged in the postwar British novel',[72] Angus Wilson was made a CBE in

1968 and knighted in 1980. Some BP workers recognised how unique a Boffin he was; one, herself a distinguished artist, had her portrait of him hung in the National Gallery:[73] 'He died recently [1991] of Alzheimer's, sadly forgotten and in much reduced circumstances.'

Alan Turing

Perhaps the most famous, mysterious, and tragic, of the BP Boffins was Alan Turing. Along with Bletchley Park's Max Newman and the GPO's Tommy Flowers, Turing has now been credited as being the father of the modern computer. His genius even then was renowned: 'We had a mathematical problem connected with probability which none of us could solve, but we were told that Turing was the man who would solve it for us, and he did.' But many remembered only his eccentricity:

'Alan Turing kept his coffee mug chained to a radiator to prevent theft . . .'

'He changed his life savings into silver ingots and buried them in Bletchley woods . . .'

'He was perpetually untidy and would fall into long silences . . .'

'His voice was most peculiar. [It] had arrested at the point where it was breaking – kept going up and back down again. Sometimes it was difficult to know what he was saying.'

'He was very shabby – in all the pictures he must have smartened up for the occasion.'

'My father [Josh Cooper] interviewed Turing before he was hired. They were walking somewhere in the streets of London [past] static water tanks, about five feet high. Turing turned to my father and said, What do you bet I can't pee into that?'

John Bowring worked for the Corps of Signals at nearby Hanslope Park. He too remembers Alan Turing's bizarre behaviour: 'He would come over to Hanslope Park from Bletchley every Tuesday . . . He was positively weird) He dressed in a way that put the average tramp to shame [wearing] his tie to hold his trousers up, and . . . a piece of rope to tie his voluminous raincoat around him as he cycled along. You could tell when he was coming as his bike was always squeaking and groaning, it was a real death trap. But he wasn't aware of that. I've seen him riding through the roads around Hanslope, in the middle of the road, his eyes not on the road at all but rather in the heavens. He was an absolute danger on the road . . .'.

However – uniquely – John Bowring also believes he can pinpoint the actual moment when Turing conceived the idea of the modern computer:)

'The lads in the workshop decided that the "Prof" ought to come and see how the other half lived. So they grabbed him on his way into the Park House and frogmarched him down to the workshops. "Now you will see the real work, Prof!" He wore his usual faraway look as he went in. One of the lads picked up a valve and said, "Now Prof, this is what we call a thermionic valve. It's an electronic device . . .". He just stood there goggle-eyed, then all of a sudden his face changed. He just sort of went rigid, stared into the middle distance, and still holding this valve in his hand, said "You know, I could make a computer with these." We think, and I certainly think, that's where the computer started . . .'

Sadly, stories of Turing have focused on the tragedy of his death rather than the significance of his achievements. Found guilty of gross indecency in 1952, he was sentenced to a course of oestrogen which caused him to grow breasts. He committed suicide by cyanide poisoning two years later. Possibly, the social hostility to what was his basic nature had been prevalent many years before – in BP: 'We used to dine opposite Alan Turing and his "girl friend". . . . It was well known that he was gay, but a brilliant chap I suppose.'

Michael Cooper concludes: 'Turing was a very anarchic soul basically and that was part of his undoing because he never concealed his sexuality. . . . My father was very upset when he heard of the suicide.'

THE DEBS

A 'Deb' (abbreviated from débutante) was a young woman from a wealthy or aristocratic British family who was presented to the reigning monarch in her first appearance to Society – her 'coming-out'. This auspicious occasion, where Debs processed up The Mall to Buckingham Palace, would mark the beginning of the London 'season' and their search for a suitable husband. The season would last from May – with parties, balls, the Derby, Ascot and the Eton–Harrow cricket match ('Lords') – until early August, ending with the Cowes Regatta. Although such events persist today, the custom of Debs being presented at Court was abolished by the Queen in 1958. Until then, Debs typically would return from the chrysalis of 'finishing school' on the Continent (with a few European languages and some artistic skills) to emerge as butterflies at their coming-out ball. Ambitious mothers ensured their daughters attended endless fittings for ball-gowns and scoured *The Times* and *The Tatler* for the list of dances to attend. It was assumed that their daughters would then successfully marry into a similar family – cosmopolitan or diplomatic perhaps. For a future ambassador's wife to be fully prepared, conversation with people who bored you was an excellent training ground. Except of course, that the war changed all that.

There was one place during the war that eligible bachelors – the next generation of Oxbridge graduates and the Establishment – could be found in abundance. Bletchley Park – 'Debs' Delight' – accordingly attracted a significant number of Debs, some drafted to BP as filing clerks: 'We were really cheap labour, to feed the Brains at BP.' But another woman saw instead the Debs' innate good fortune 'because they usually had their own transport. But they were very nice people . . .'.

Sketches of colleagues from Hut 3 1941–3, by
Naomi Holme née Phillips (BPTA 62):
a. Betsy Arbuthnot
b. Marion Kirkpatrick
c. Joyce Parkes
d. Anne Harrison
e. Joy Buirtes(?)

There was a sense of shared endeavour, however: 'The drivers [included] Lady Jean Graham, Lady Rowsbotham and Dianne Sou – all volunteers. They weren't in uniform and we were the only two ATS. But they did exactly the same job as us.'

Some Debs, trapped abroad when conflict loomed, had perilous escapes – possibly subject matter for the 'James Bond' stories: 'We had to leave our flat in Milan shortly after it was taken over by Mussolini's Blackshirts. We were on the last train to leave Lyons. . . . We slept on the floor in Bordeaux station screened by our suitcases . . . [and] on the dunes of the Gironde, waiting for a boat to take us to England. Finally, we came on a cargo boat to Falmouth commandeered by Ian Fleming . . .'.

They were also recruited direct from universities – at home and abroad: 'I was bilingual in French and English and studied German. I had lived in Paris, Bruxelles and Holland and had a small private allowance.'

When these highly educated, sophisticated young women were working alongside other 'geese', a class chasm emerged which even BP could not bridge: 'I was given four or five girls as copy-typists. One said when I was interviewing her, "Well, me name's Maudie, but I like being called Queenie. I did used to work at Fletton's but then I thought I'd better meself so I threw up the brickworks and went into the Co-op. . .". Another said [of Italian agents] "They've got a good opinion of themselves haven't they? Always saying Fine message." *Fine messagio* meant "the end of the message". They didn't appear to have any idea of what they were doing and talked steadily about boyfriends and rationing and clothes coupons as they typed . . .'.

In contrast, the description by one Deb of her decoding room recalls the refinement of her cultural background: 'Codes were named after musical instruments forming an Orchestra. The conductor sat in the centre, entering lists of cracks on a large cardboard sheet, distributing them to other interested "instruments" and phoning them up to Cheadle. I was allotted to "Mandolin", my mentor being a very knowledgeable, courteous Russian refugee named Paul Fetterlin . . .'.

Some Debs did progress beyond 'feeding the Brains' to head a section: 'The lady who was in charge of us all was Blades Spotford . . . who was inclined to wear jangly earrings and scarves.' However most Debs who were remembered were cited as friends or acquaintances rather than for their work contributions:

'I knew a charming girl called Sally Norton who became Lady Astor. Her friend Osla Benning was a Canadian whose boyfriend at that time was Prince Philip. Then Osla met another man (whom she married) and broke it off with Philip – I remember teasing her about becoming a Greek princess. Then there was Jeanie Campbell-Harris, now Baroness Trumpington . . .'

'One person I played tennis with was Janna Wambeek – her father was a Group Captain. I knew Georgina and Doris Molle – they had fled to England from Belgium. Also Sigonia Guessons and Grizzelda Robarts – her father was a merchant banker.'

'I'd brought my wife down with me, which was a bit of a mistake of course as I later got very keen on one of the girls here – Miss Rosamunde Pilcher actually. A beautiful girl who was the daughter of Gladys Cooper and Richard Merrivale and who is now a well-known novelist. Happy days!'

Famous men like Alvar Lidell, the quintessential BBC Radio Announcer, were singled out as contributing to 'the lofty atmosphere of the place'. Few woman were remembered thus. An exception was 'Audrey Element – the first western woman ever to enter Tibet on a yak'.

CHAPTER 8
Service Personnel

'The day before my demobilisation, I had to go and see Colonel J. He was very kind to me, gave me a talk on security and then produced a Bible. I had to put my hand on it and swear I would never divulge anything that was secret. Then I signed the Official Secrets Act and relinquished my pass into BP. He shook hands with me and wished me good luck. I saluted and said goodbye.'

At a meeting held at Bletchley Park on 23 March 1942, the Head of BP, Commander Travis, endeavoured to appease some visiting leaders of the armed forces. He explained that the sole preoccupation of BP '*now*' was to '*serve*' the three fighting Services, 'which was rather different from the position at the time of the last BP meeting. . . . He hoped the three Service Ministries would always tell us exactly how we could be of most help to them . . .'.

Certainly, for the 'geese', collaboration seemed to operate both between the Services and with Foreign Office (FO) civilians. One woman working in the Decoding Room reckoned that personnel were '60% WRENs, 30% FO, 10% ATS'. Another commented on the consequent relaxation of Service regulations: 'There were so many different uniforms . . . so we were instructed there was to be no saluting while on base. Which could cause difficulties when we omitted to salute while off base . . .'.

Unknown officer at Bletchley Park. Pencilled note on the back of the photo says:
'2.1.40...
Para A. Please give early instructions re Fiddes.
B. I don't want to appear too pressing, but unless some action taken. Trawler Owners...'
(BPTA P204)

'*The assortment of personnel at Bletchley Park*'; and '*Intelligence Officers*'; cartoons by D. Hukton. (BPTA 21)

However, there were serious misgivings in the Services about how they were apparently being exploited by BP: 'I am disturbed by your statement that it is your intention to fill all future vacancies by WAAF personnel and that you have gone so far as to encourage likely civilian candidates to join the WAAF before coming to you. . . . This question of the employment of service personnel in duties which can be performed by civilians is one on which very decided views are held in high quarters and it is necessary for us to ensure that this method of filling posts is only resorted to when all other means have failed.'[74]

There was a canny reason for such recruiting machinations at Bletchley Park, but it was not for ordinary Service men and women to reason why or how they were at BP. They just had to follow orders.

THE ARMY

The men

'The Army people wore Intelligence Corps insignia, described to me by one of them as "a pansy resting on its laurels". Indeed I was to find that there were quite a few of those[75] and very charming they were.'

It was an odd world that new army recruits found themselves in. The unique assortment of BP personnel – and the lack of any structure to suit them – resulted in an unconventional use of Army ranks: 'I was promoted from Private to Company Sergeant Major in eight months. It was simply a way of ensuring that I was given more pay as well as greater privileges in the camp – for example the Sergeants' Mess was greatly superior.'

The oddity developed as the norm at BP but with idiosyncratic routines: '[I was] temporarily a Service officer . . . we wore uniform only if we felt like it or when some top brass was expected on a visit . . .'. There were arbitrary classifications: 'If you came in as a civilian, not from the forces, then you were given some kind of rank. For example Asa Briggs was a private. Immediately at the end of the war he became Director of BBC Broadcasting for the Services. It was a curious situation because there was no respect paid to rank.'

'Regular army' men found this very difficult to accept, particularly Colonel Fillingham, Commander of the Shenley Road Military Camp next to Bletchley Park:

'Lt Col Fillingham was not privy to the work of BP but was in administrative charge of the camp in which we as Army personnel lived. His was an impossible position – any army-type requirement he tried to impose on his recalcitrant inmates could always be thwarted by our disappearing to the 'office' on 'important business'. He was not a flexible man – his demands were often not in keeping with our perception of our priorities. The relationship was not a happy one . . .'

'He was a dapper little man with a neatly trimmed moustache and extremely shrewd, snapping boot-button eyes . . . a martinet . . .'

'BP authorities naturally regarded us as their people who happened to be living in an army camp, while for the officers in charge of the camp, we were a funny lot of soldiers who were doing some peculiar job or other. The sight of some soldiers – as they shambled about, uniforms awry, caps at strange angles and badges and boots uncleaned – must have galled the CO, Colonel Fillingham, deeply. From time to time, goaded beyond endurance he would explode with rage . . . [He] did what he could to keep us up to some sort of military scratch and to repel the egalitarianism and informality of BP . . .'

From the point of view of brain-weary code-breakers returning from BP shift-work, the imposition of Army regulations became a running sore: 'PT was a regular nuisance: when I was on the day shift, I was obliged to rise early and jump about. . . . More troublesome was "Military Training". This involved assault courses, running about the countryside pretending to be engaged in battle. [BP] thought it was a waste of our time, but much more seriously that it was liable to exhaust us before we started work. Protests were made [and] we were given special dispensation . . .'.

Notwithstanding these extraordinary tensions, normal army life persisted with plenty of incident to fuel daily gossip – for example, the Scandal of the Sheets: 'Over 200 sheets provided for ATS women were stolen from the stores. There was much excitement, and Military Police swarmed over the Camp. The culprits turned out to be several General Duties (GD) men who rapidly disappeared to the detention barracks . . .'. This particular reminiscence adds a unique and sympathetic insight into the lives of these lowly servicemen:

'GD men were a depressed class, the very bottom of the totem pole. They had been drafted to the Camp from Infantry regiments, where because of medical unfitness, misconduct, or total incompetence, they had been classed as unable to perform more honourable service. They acted as permanent 'fatigue' men, carrying out all the sweeping, cleaning and similar jobs as well as providing a nominal guard for the Camp . . .'

'Until I was promoted to Sergeant, I lived in a hut with a number of GD men and found their straightforward pursuit of drink and sex – their sole interests – a sometimes refreshing change from the Testery[76] where drink and sex were also pursued but in a much more cerebral atmosphere. . . . BP workers were excused the periodic ritual of the FFI inspection (Free From Infection) in which we used to lower our trousers before the Medical Officer while he (or she at the Camp) peered accusingly into the murky recesses of our private parts. GD men remained subject to this humiliation. Not that FFIs seemed to do much good. I recall one of the Durham Light Infantry Geordies coming into our hut one evening, scratching himself extensively and complaining to anyone who cared to listen, "Me fookin' crabs is fookin' terrible tonight."'

The Release Leave Certificate from the army for Harold Monkton. (BPTA 60)

Corporal Eric de Carteret who 'manned Room 3 of Block D, down the corridor in a very small room, like a large stationery cupboard where we went for spare pencils, paper, etc. . . . He came from the Channel Islands. . . . I was highly suspicious of him as he had, I thought, a German accent at times, and my great-aunt disappeared at the time of the German occupation.' The photograph, signed by Cpl de Carteret is inscribed: 'To Mr, Mrs and Bessie Goodwin in appreciation of their kindness to me during my happy stay in Bletchley, May 1942–1945.' Cpl de Carteret also took photo stills for the BP Drama Group – see page 96. (BPTA 50)

The women – The ATS (Auxiliary Territorial Service)

'I was a very ordinary ATS officer who was engaged in purely administrative duties and in no way one of the brilliant brains who did so much to shorten the war.'

Many ATS drivers worked at BP: 'I drove a Colonel and Major to Chatsworth House and stayed overnight in Leicester. One stayed at the Bell Hotel and the other at the Bull Hotel near Beaumanor and I was over the road at the ATS place. In the morning I checked on the car – petrol, water – and then picked them both up and went on to where the big meeting was. We stayed there all day and came back to Bletchley Park.'

Interestingly, 'there were quite a lot of ATS daughters of clergymen', but whatever the background 'the wheezes we got up to, to get out of doing PT. We were supposed to do it twice a week even in the bitterly cold. We would go and chat up – distract – the person who checked us in and out . . .'.

However, one ATS officer at the Shenley Road camp echoed the tensions suffered by Colonel Fillingham with whom she had considerable sympathy:

'[There were some] Junior officers who were probably good at their work at BP . . . but once they returned to camp they became grudging and mean-minded, resentful towards administrative officers, and quite disagreeable towards one another. . . . None of them was a senior officer, and possibly the work they did at BP was of a routine and soul-destroying nature, which may have caused them to become embittered. The fact remains they dragged their feet and gave the impression that they regarded us (the HQ officers) as the enemy. They made life for us as difficult as they could by making snide and infuriating comments and by grumbling and complaining non-stop – not openly but usually in a loud voice as one passed by, followed by malicious sniggers. I always completely ignored it.'

THE NAVY

The men

'We had a Chief Petty Officer Banford who was good with electrical equipment. He taught me to swear as he often got shocks testing the equipment.'

All senior staff officers in the three Services were asked, when visiting Bletchley, to come in mufti.[77] The Army and RAF concurred but not the Navy – they insisted in keeping their uniform: 'What the people working at Bletchley Station thought of all these incredibly handsome and marvellously uniformed senior admiralty bods I simply don't know.'

The Navy's determination sometimes misfired however: 'An order came down from on high that as we were officers we better damn well do some training. So there was an enemy group and a British group and we played around in the grounds of the mansion as though we had been invaded. The defending group had to stop the "enemy" getting through the wires. The attacking group dug a hole under the wire and captured the place in about 10 minutes. I joined in with a tennis sweater on and was killed in the first few minutes.'

The women – Women's Royal Naval Service (Wrens)

'I joined the Navy to see the sea and what did I see? I saw BP.'

It is the Navy's female branch – the Wrens – that has produced most of this service's reminiscence about BP, perhaps unsurprisingly when there were around 3,000 of them engaged on its work. The first Wrens arrived early in 1941: 'By 1942, any doubts that they could undertake the work with Alan Turing's Bombes were dispelled – they replaced men and their category was allocated as "Special Duties X".'

Many of them ended up in Hut 11: 'The machine room was staffed almost entirely by Wrens except for the PO technicians; in the front were half a dozen trestle tables as well as Newman's own office which was on a slightly raised platform.' They were supervised by 'the Queen Bee of the Bletchley Park Wrens': 'Petty Officer Zoë Zuppinger,[78] a charming girl . . . She was of course ancient – she must have been at least 23.'

I say, little Wren, when, when, when
   Will you next have a moment to be free?
I mean, little Wren, when, when, when,
   Will you please do some typing for me?
Let's go into your den; you take up your pen;
   Here's a note for Bentley — do it there and then.
But more, little Wren! — seeing it's so near the en'
   I would say thanks for all the work you've done for me.

                                                    Willie Ewing
                                                    20.10.45

Handwritten verse penned in appreciation of the Wrens by Willie Ewing (see also group photo on page 67). (BPTA)

But despite their acknowledged worth, Wrens still encountered a 'glass ceiling' obstructing their promotion and imposing on them, almost without exception, male bosses: 'I only ever met one female officer and she had done similar work as a civilian'; 'I was placed in the RR[79] in an all-female section headed by a businessman called Harold Fletcher.' Even male accoutrements were discouraged in women: 'We were only allowed to wear slacks on night watch . . .'.

A woman's role was typically seen as servicing the needs of other, more important members of staff. One [male] decoder recalls: 'My group had about 20 senior staff, and about 300–400 Wrens who did secretarial work for us.' A Wren wryly comments: 'We could make tea or coffee and of course the Wrens did that and handed it out to the elite, the linguists.'

Sometimes the effects of male prejudice would produce a little female rancour: 'We women – mainly in routine jobs and occasionally having to cope with what would now be called sexual harassment from a few of the men – often viewed some of the men involved in administrative work with a certain amount of cynicism.'

Gordon Preston recalled a time when he urged a different approach to that traditionally adopted by male colleagues:

'The Wrens did a great deal of work on "rectangling" – a method of trying to get very small messages decoded by hand. This seemed a ludicrous waste of effort. The Wrens all had to have a qualification in mathematics – quite a number with Honours Degrees – and here we were asking them to do mathematical jobs without explaining it. I managed to persuade Newman that it would pay off if they knew what it was all about. He had the attitude that "women wouldn't like to do any intellectual work". He didn't think any of them would come along. Well, I advertised it . . . Every Wren took part in these energetic lectures and the output was considerably improved as a result.'

Of course the 'glass ceiling' became more of a fixture when women themselves were prepared to fit the traditional mould: 'A lot of code breaking was based on instinct – that's probably why women were so good at it – you had to follow your

Bletchley Park Wrens 1943-1945. Featured are Mollie Siddell, Isle of Man; Freda Tootal, Manchester; Margaret Lewesley, Manchester; Margaret Stocker, Birmingham; Beryl Thomas, Rhyl; Barbara Marquiss, Leeds; Dina Markwick, Scotland; Joyce Bringloe, Sutton Valence; Bobby Valence, Barry, South Wales. (BPTA)

hunches.'; 'I have to admit that my choice of Service was partly influenced by the fact that khaki would have done very little for mousy hair and a sallow complexion . . .'.

For the most part however, Wrens carried on regardless and uncomplaining, despite condescending gestures: 'Once Admiral Cunningham patted me on the back I know not why!' In fact, the overwhelming tone of their reminiscences is one of cheerful gratitude and companionship: 'We used to get cigarettes issued to us very cheaply. We didn't get a rum ration, they gave us two pence instead – I used to drink pink gin', and 'the really nice thing was that the girls we worked with were all wonderful.'

There is also a strong sense of indignation in those whose loyal service was undermined, they felt, by the indiscretion of others: 'One day I came home on leave my father said, I know what you are doing – you are breaking German codes. I asked him how he found out and he said Admiral G, Head of Naval Intelligence, had told him. I cannot describe how angry I was. We little Wrens were able to keep our mouths shut, and yet a man of such eminence of Admiral G could tell my father. Anyway that is all behind us . . .'. One anecdote reveals just how strong that feeling of outrage was, even many years after the war:

'Gordon Welchman's[80] father, Canon Welchman had married my parents. When I visited him in my Wren uniform he asked where I was working. Thinking this dear old man would never know it, I told him I was working at a small place called Bletchley. "Do you mean Bletchley Park?" he said. "Oh my goodness, what have I said?" So I had to admit it was. "My son Gordon who had a first class honours degree in Mathematics at Cambridge, he's working at Bletchley Park on very secret and important secret business." When I got back on leave and I thought this was great – I walked into the Watch and said, "Does anyone know where Gordon Welchman works in the Park?" They all looked up at me from what they were doing with stern looks and stony silence, and then went back to what they were doing . . . When I related this story at a dinner to launch Channel 4's *Station X*, one man overhearing it thumped the table and said, "I hope you reported the Archdeacon and I hope he was thrown into prison for the rest of the war!"'

THE AIR FORCE

'I don't remember meeting anyone famous in those days, but I knew and worked with other nice WAAFs.'

The Air Force, like the Army, had physical lines drawn between those in charge at BP (the men) and those beneath them (the women):

'Right by the side of the door into the Auto Room was an elevated glass-walled room, occupied by the officers in charge of the watch . . .'

'The Royal Air Force or The Glamour Boys' – cartoon by D. Hukton. (BPTA 21)

'We think that the section above the steps was where the 'big decisions were made'. We were not allowed up there.'

The 'girls' were called upon only if perceived to be useful to the men: 'They kept a lookout for the girls they thought may be able to help them . . .'.

The WAAF (Women's Auxiliary Air Force) was largely employed in the more mundane wireless – or radio – work at BP: 'with occasional flurries of excitement, but the people one worked with were tremendous fun'. The wireless room itself was entirely staffed by WAAFs with 'a couple of RAF technicians to service the sets'. All the officers in charge were RAF, most of them ex-'Cable and Wireless' men. Perhaps the most revealing reminiscence of the tedium WAAFs experienced in working for them is in an anonymous 'Doggerel written on Watch when bored':

> 'I hope that I shall never see
> A thing I hate more heartily –
> A wireless set which squeaks and then
> Just squeaks and squeaks and squeaks again.
> A set that makes you swear and frown,
> A set whose note goes up and down
> And eats up dots and dashes too
> Then spews the whole thing back at you
> Poems are made by fools like me
> But only hell makes things like thee . . .'

One WAAF noted in her diary the modest pleasures that lightened the routine:

'Monday 4th January 1943: Fire in room – glorious! . . .
Thursday 7th Jan: Stayed in bed till 10! Cleaned up – pay parade 12.30
Soap coupon! . . .
Sat. 23rd Jan: Tea, custard powder and salad cream from auntie . . .'

However, her entries are also infused with anxieties and tensions familiar to anyone who has experienced corporate life where you have no control over what you have to do:

'Sat 29th May 1943: Nothing exciting . . . shall I stick to job? . . .
Frid 4th June: 9–6 Capt M in bad mood . . .
Tues 8 June: 4–12 Busy day, for a change! . . .
Thurs 10 June: 9–6 Nothing exciting . . . had to work my day's off – what a to-do – coward!. . .'

Another WAAF, doubtless also bored while on night shift, wrote an insider's guide on 'How to court a Radio girl':

'If she wants a date – meter
If she comes to call – receiver
If she wants an escort – conductor

'WAAFs at RAF Station, Church Green Bletchley, courtesy LACW Kent – 'I am the one with hands in front and crossed'. (BPTA P279.012 and .013)

If she wants to be an angel – transformer
If she proves you wrong – compensator
If she thinks you a cheat – detector
If she eats too much – rectifier
If her hands are cold – heater
If she wants a vacation – transmitter
If she talks too much – interrupter
If she's narrow in her view – amplifier
If she wants to be true – eliminator.'

FRATERNISATION

'The Americans were brought in after Pearl Harbour in 1941. They were a charming group of people and we worked very happily with them.'

In 1945 there were 233 members of the US Forces recorded working at Bletchley Park. The cooperation between the two nations grew, fuelled by the freshness of the newcomers' approach: 'There were a couple of Americans, full of enthusiasm. One was called Al. His birthday was in March – we bought him a cake.'

Sometimes relationships blossomed, then unhappily died. The following anonymous verse came off a teleprinter during a slack period of the night shift at BP on 7 July 1944, and was kept by the Wren receiving it, possibly as a cautionary reminder about American liaisons:

Hut 128, RAF Church Green. LACW West (later Mrs Caroline Shearer) is 2nd front right. (BPTA P349)

'You are their life, their love, their all
And for no other would they fall
They'll love you dear, till death do part
If you leave them, you'll break their heart
And they leave you broken hearted
The camp has moved your love departed
You wait for mail that doesn't come
Then you realise you're awful dumb
In a different town
A different place
To a different girl
A different face
"I love you darling, please be mine"
It's the same old Yank
The same old line.'

It was inevitable that BP's mix of different Services and ranks would result in unconventional groupings. 'If we were lucky we'd maybe sit next to Naval, Army or RAF Officers, some of them with impressive scrambled egg on their uniforms. One Wren remembered: 'an old rowing boat and one or two of our RAF technicians would occasionally take us out until it looked like sinking . . . '.

One man however was 'particularly annoyed' by the insistence of a Commanding Officer to interfere in his liaison with one of the ATS officers in charge of the machine room at the Testery: 'I do not recall anyone at BP thinking it strange or commenting on the disparity when I as a Private began to go out regularly with a female officer. But eyebrows were certainly raised in the Camp.'

CHAPTER 9
The Civilian Division

'It seemed to be the hive of activity with all sorts of people there, men and women, some in uniform – high rank or low, all mixing together, and civilians all thrown into one big melting pot.'

The 'higher echelons' of civilians were cryptanalysts and compilers of records of the whole enemy war machine. Others included interpreters, linguists, cipher clerks, teleprinter operators, telephonists – 'an enormous support group of technical and clerical people', 'mostly women, thousands actually, who paved the way for the "Brains". I was one of these women, a tiny cog in a fantastic wheel!' Mingling with the Wrens and ATS were civilians from 'quite a mixture' of backgrounds. In addition to contacting 'a lot of graduates from the smaller universities' there was a search for people with particular skills: 'my wife was a PO operator. As there was a shortage of operators at that time, she was contacted and accepted a position.' At times it was almost a family business: 'We were the two youngest in Hut 8 and called the babies. I had various cousins also with me. My sister (in Mechanised Transport) drove us to and from the Park.

Those in the armed forces often saw BP civilians as a group apart: 'There were important-looking civilians who completely ignored us Wrens, the humblest of all.' Service women, for example, would 'always' have 'a man in charge of the Watch. . . . They were quite young men but all very clever, but they just all fell asleep and we had to wake them if anything significant came off the machines.'

Even those who were themselves in a supervisory position felt threatened by what they perceived as civilians' 'assumption of superiority'. One ATS officer commented bitterly: 'Their brains were overdeveloped to the detriment of their personalities. This led to an atmosphere of egotism, not to mention spitefulness and backbiting. The precept of public service was unknown to them and though they would do what they were paid to do, the thought of doing a bit more did not occur to them. There was no generosity of spirit, no feeling of loyalty to the unit as is the case in, for instance, an infantry regiment. I expect they were unhappy and took it out on us but some of them treated the Mess staff abominably and made it quite clear that they considered themselves superior to the rest of us.'

Indeed, some service personnel felt aggrieved that their hardships were simply not appreciated – 'discipline was very strict' – whereas life for civilians seemed exclusive and jolly, in an elitist sort of way: 'A small earnest group of civilians would perform country dances in their breaks on fine days, on the lawn near the

lake'; 'civilians were the ones that seemed to use the tennis courts or sit around the lake having picnics.'

For their part, erstwhile civilians who found themselves in the Army 'for the duration' because of their work at BP had their own crosses to bear: 'One knew absolutely nothing about the Army, or parading or anything. It was a very difficult time because we had to go through the motions and waste our time when we – at least I – was anxious to get back and do something worthwhile . . .'.

However, some civilians found being in the services a decided advantage: 'Before I was commissioned in the camp I remember great big huts with all of us sleeping in them but when you became commissioned you had a little cubicle to yourself.'

Interestingly, many civilian reminiscences reveal an equal sense of being a very unimportant cog. Apart from their work group, there was not much connection with others at BP: 'Unless there were family ties, we (civilians) had no contact with other huts and did not participate in any plays or concerts or dances.' Even at work the disposition of others emphasised the division: 'The men who came in and stood over us trying to solve the codes were mostly higher Army officers or older men . . .'.

The sense of isolation could also emerge from within a particular work section: 'The other girls refused to work with me as I was getting through much more than they were. The team-leader went to see Mr Freeman who called me into his office and said, I want you to take charge of that team. He then came out and wiped the floor with the girls. Mind you, I had only been there about three weeks.'

For one hapless newcomer, there was animosity before she even started: 'My first few working days were pure hell. . . . Someone had told the room where I started work that I was coming from the FO to tell them how to do their work. I walked into an atmosphere of such pure hostility that I spent a large part of my time crying in the loo.'

Even within commonly respected working areas ('Hut 6 was the elite one') civilian workers saw themselves as subservient and 'humble' – 'poor relations' who could not enter 'forbidden territory': 'We lesser mortals in WTI[81] communicated with next door through a hatch, but never dreamed of entering the sacred precinct'; 'I was a very unimportant cog!'

Being a civilian 'insider' at BP – not obviously working for the war effort like

uniformed colleagues – brought further problems with the reactions of people outside: 'Locals looked down on us as "rich" or "upper class", evaders of war while their relatives went into services or munitions – uncomfortable at the time as one could not defend oneself from those taunts.' Misunderstanding was common: 'I remember a Major Doolittle coming to us in the Park while I was there. . . . Friends said, That's a good name. Because we couldn't tell them what we did, they thought we were lazy layabouts who didn't do anything.'

Even fellow workers at BP distrusted their motives. A security officer's report to Commander Denniston referred to 'civil employees who have dodged out of London either to avoid the air raids or being called upon for Military service.'[82]

There were other difficulties for civilians: one 'didn't take to communal living'; another grumpily recorded she was 'compulsorily moved' to another section. The sense of isolation, thought one officer, perhaps came from their urban upbringing: 'Probably most of the people at Bletchley were more orientated towards the town than the country and felt that they were miserably marooned in a wilderness. I was country born and bred and had everyday skills and knowledge that were second nature to me. I doubt if most of them could have named the various trees and birds or wildflowers around us. Certainly some of them were afraid of cattle. . .' .

There were happier anecdotes, however: 'I was very, very lucky with the girls there. I landed with a group of girls who couldn't be nicer'; 'We were billeted in Stony Stratford with Lord Harwood. He would chauffeur us to the Park and would stop at a pub on the way back.'

And at times there was great resourcefulness: 'When the Government was looking for somewhere to process the card-index system, people from two firms had to give a public demonstration. Our BTM[83] man suddenly realised that he hadn't brought the paper. He ran into the Gents' cloakroom and got a toilet roll and used that . . . and won the contract!'

Both pages: Co-workers at the Foreign Office in Block E, December 1943 – August 1945. Featured are from top left opposite, left to right: Doreen, Joan, Mary, Kathleen, Doris, Tegwyn, Doris, Sylvia, Beryl, Lilian, Freda, Marjorie, Christine. (BPTA)

CHAPTER 10

Food and Entertainment

'C is for Crawley – our own dietician
Who serves up our grub like a mathematician
It's round stodge or square for the rest of your life
And eat the darned stuff without even a knife . . .

Y is for You, folks in the Hall
As time passes by I hope you'll recall
The dances you've been to here – above all
Tonight the Japanese Victory Ball!'

Because of wartime food rationing[84] BP catering had its limitations; but it was impressively large-scale. By January 1945 nearly 25,000 meals a week were served around the clock. At first, operations had been modest: 'We would come into the Mansion to eat. Everyone was in this little mess room together.'

But a burgeoning workforce required more, and diners removed to the hall: 'It was the first time in my life I had ever had cafeteria-style food which was unusual then.'

Then they built the canteen: 'Inside the BP big gates on the left was my favourite dive when on duty. . . . The huge canteen was a meeting place both for meals and functions. The food was really quite good.'

One local woman worked there: 'It was very hard. There was a very large boiler to cook puddings and vegetables which we helped prepare. Also lots of sandwiches – dried egg, spam[85] and salad etc.'

The best efforts of canteen staff were not always enjoyed however:

'Personally I could not swallow the sponge puddings which emerged from long metal containers. They were pale yellow (bogus vanilla), bright pink ("rose" scent flavour), mauve ("violet" scented – ugh) and brown (cocoa – and just edible if one was really hungry). The "custard" sloshed over them helped to get them down to some extent.'

'Our canteen outshone any sleazy restaurant. The smell of watery cabbage and stale fat afflicted us to the point of nausea. One day I found a cooked cockroach nestling in my meat. I was about to return it to the catering manager when Osla who had the appetite of a lioness with cubs snatched it off the plate and said,

'What a waste! I'll eat it.'

'Frozen meat and terrible 'cardboard' tarts . . .'

'The BP canteen did at least have access to 'home-grown' meat.'

'There were pig-sties down by the pumping station. I'd feed the pigs with pigswill – only about 5 I think. They were killed and cured to help feed the people.'

It also provided hot meals through the night:

'Kidneys on toast at 3am on night shift – I shudder at the thought 58 years later.'

'They did their best, though, these people. I really think they did their best.'

In November 1944 the WRNS Cafeteria opened at BP serving 1,000 meals a day at its peak. You had to have 'the requisite meal ticket' and your pass to be allowed back in: 'What a long way we had to walk from Block G to the cafeteria, just outside the main gates, especially during the night shift when we went over there at 2.30am–3am and again for breakfast at 7.30am in pitch dark – no lights were allowed.'
And sometimes, you wondered whether it was worth the effort:

'Suppers on the night shift were a particular pleasure (but) the food was pretty terrible – for want of anything better, I used to eat quantities of beetroot . . .'

'At 3am they would feed us corned beef and prunes. I've never touched either since.'

'Baked beans for breakfast after night duty (ugh).'

However, many were grateful for the fare they were offered there:

'The food was excellent. I put on quite a lot of weight.'

'We got real coffee – it came in those sealed tins, Lyons I think.'

'Woolton Pie I remember best, a sort of cheese and onion pie.'

'A lot of people complained about the meals but I thought they were wonderful.'

Rations improved 'when the Americans came over':

'You would find yourself sitting next to an American Colonel or whoever; there was no rank difference. The Americans seemed to eat everything with a fork – even rice pudding.'

One American officer commented on the difference between BP offerings and his other meals: 'The food was not as good as any at Little Brickhill[86] [but] I was addicted to the toast of off-white bread then made in Britain and could always swap for some when kippers were on the breakfast menu. The Britons were hungry for protein and it was a delight to see the English girls attack my kipper with vigor while I ate their toast. . . . We had three great cooks. Ernie the baker from Philadelphia would turn out delicious pastries made from scratch and produced passable omelets from powdered eggs. . . . Our rations came daily from the air base and surpassed by far anything the British could offer or sell at the time.'

Fond memories of the WVS[87] canteen on Bletchley Station open from early morning until late at night include:

'[the] magnificent meal of sausage, egg and chips at a very reasonable price.'

'We used to take it in turns to go down to the Station each morning to get a jug of tea and a dozen hot, buttered rolls.'

'They gave of their time voluntarily enabling all service men and women to have refreshments at a busy rail junction – just for pennies.'

To visit WVS was an opportunity, like for truanting schoolchildren, to cock a snook at the rules: 'We would sneak out by that path around the lake behind the Sick Bay and go to the railway station where we could buy cider and cakes – we were supposed to go out by the path by the main gate.'

It was essential for 'geese' survival to be able to obtain snacks and tea, as well as other beverages such as beer: 'Q is for tea – it is only a penny. . . But if there is cake, it stretches to Fenny . . .'[88]

The choice for where to have a cup of 'Rosie Lee'[89] ranged from the lounge area of the main house (where 'some of us belonged to the coffee club') to a couple of on-site snack bars. Hut 2[90] supplied beverages, snacks, and beer – and also sold luncheon vouchers.[91]

The NAAFI stores, by the 'Coffee Hut', was 'a kiosk/cabin type structure made of wood with a flap at the front, lowered when open for business – which was only when stock came in'. Then, you could buy '2oz bars of Ration Chocolate wrapped in grease-proof paper in red or blue – plain or milk; cigarettes, tobacco, lighters, fountain pens, (these last two very occasionally); large bottles of Camp coffee and "NAAFI" cake of a Madeira type. You could also get bags of broken chocolate or biscuits.'

Sometimes there were 'rare treats':

'single pieces of fruit cake . . .'

GROUPIE.
(SCRAMBLED EGG & FRUIT SALAD!)

Cartoon of 'Groupie' by D. Hukton
(BPTA 21)

Snack hut for the Teachers' Training College at Bletchley Park in 1948. The TTC were the first long-term users of BP post war, followed in mid-1948 by the Diplomatic Wireless Service and the Ministry of Civil Aviation. The Poles (Polish Displaced Persons) left in 1948 and the Control Commission for Germany left in late 1947 (BPTA 99.028.007)

'cosmetics and soap. Rarer still, small bars of chocolate, usually Fuller's Cream Bars – just one each.'

The 'Tuck cabin' was 'manned by a sailor who sat knitting between sales':

> 'D is for Denny[92] whose nickname is "Stoker"
> We think 'cos he peps up his pipe with a poker . . .'

If work was too demanding to leave even for a moment, 'geese' had their break in their work area. But this had its drawbacks, namely:

'Navy biscuits that had to be soaked for ages in cocoa before you could attempt to eat them.'

'the most ghastly "brews" to keep awake, mixed with dried milk. It was very hard to make a decent drink without great lumps.'

'terrible green tea and hard buns that would break if you dropped them on the floor . . .'

'such revolting food as cheese and piccalilli in the middle of the night . . .'

'a delicacy: bread-and-dripping sandwiches.'

'It was at BP that for the first and last time I ate whale meat!'

There were culinary pleasures too, though. One joyful diary entry proclaims: 'Wed 10 Feb: Egg for breakfast!'
Other anecdotes refer to local hostelries that served highly palatable dishes:

'Ox-heart, at a price, at the Station Inn, if in luck . . .'

'On Fridays a whole crowd of us would go to a delightful pub just outside the perimeter of the Park[93] where the publican's wife used up her week's jam ration to make a baked jam roll – simply delicious.'

The Lake, also, was a great focal point:

'After lunch in the summer we'd take our cups of tea or coffee down by the lake. Very peaceful. The war seemed far away.'

'For the night shift, we would fill the jug from a barrel of beer (in our billet) and bring it back down and row on the lake.'

Sometimes, wearied of wartime deprivation, friends would combine their gourmet talents for a special occasion, although not always with unqualified

BPRC membership card and information. From Kay Pickett née Harrison. (BPTA 18)

success: 'We decided to have a party. We would all contribute something. I offered to make a potato salad – I used to make mayonnaise at home so I knew how to do that. A friend said she'd get some olive oil from London. We didn't have real eggs, so I made it with powdered egg. My friend forgot to bring the olive oil, so I decided to use liquid paraffin. I mixed it all up, but it didn't look very convincing, so I put some Lemsip in and some salt . . . Everybody said how good it was and ate the lot. The next day they were all queuing up to use the loos – the liquid paraffin was quite effective!'

OFF-DUTY TIME

'I always enjoyed watching the others in the cafeteria. We saw Generals Montgomery, Alexander, Eisenhower, many Admirals . . . There were WAAFs, ATS, weedy-looking young men, all sorts. We were known by locals as the Human Whipsnade . . .'

Initially, the main house was the only indoor venue for off-duty activities:

'The huts were very bare (so) we would retire to the big house. . . . It housed the library, and a large downstairs lounge where you could have coffee, listen to music and talk.'

'We could book the bathroom in the house once a fortnight. It was a study in mahogany, the bath massive with a great metal plug. The lavatory was a real throne – up a few steps, and a work of art. I loved those bath times.'

ATS off duty!
From Gladys
Sweetland.
(BPTA P357.002)

But of course, there were also the grounds to stroll in, and the lake to enjoy:

'Big white geese would frighten the life out of the girls taking a narrow footpath to the huts. They would stand on the bank hissing so the girls always waited until there was a number of men going their way.'

'At night, frogs from the lake would descend onto the drive – being the blackout, one often trod on one.'

'The big thing about the lake was taking the boat out and getting stuck on the island. I was never fortunate enough to be stuck with anyone interesting – just a couple of girls from the office.'

Or you could improvise: 'Sometimes on a cold day we'd sit on the bus at lunch-time listening to Fats Waller records on this old wind-up gramophone.'
One WAAF diary records highlights of being off-duty during the ration era:

'Sat 16th Jan: Bought cocoa, milk, lemon crystals and Lux! . . .
Friday 16th April: Went for a short ride – came to grief on a hill, arrived back OK. Darned stockings and packed. . . .
Wed 1st Sept: Day off – shopped – chocolate and nail varnish!'

Similarly, a fellow serviceman recalls 'getting Brylcream for one of the Duty Officers. You got it on your ration and I didn't want it . . . '.
For the traditionally minded, Sunday lunchtimes included a half-hour's service in St Mary's, next to BP: 'A small choir from BP helped with the singing – psalms, canticles, and hymns, perhaps a short anthem . . . I recall the tiny pews we women sat on; they were the appropriate size for little choirboys!'
But in the early days, recreational choices were limited:

'I went for walks, chatted with friends, didn't go to pubs or drink or anything – rather a dull kind of life. I read a good deal – probably what most of us did.'

'Friday 12th November: Hitched to the 'Fountain' – grand lunch and gin & orange. Laughed a lot – good fun – hitched back. Lilly + officer! Letter from Doris + 18 fags . . .'

'Getting cigarettes was a hell of a job even in our NAAFI, plenty of American cigarettes of course. To a proper cigarette smoker, American cigarettes aren't much good.'

'We all smoked . . .'

As numbers increased, more dedicated facilities were needed – like the 'Bath Hut':[94] 'I sometimes didn't have lunch but had a bath and hair-wash in the Bath Hut. Needless to say plugs disappeared, so you had to stuff up the plug-hole and hope for the best. The hair dryers rarely worked . . . '.

However, one of the unique features of BP – memories of which endure for many 'geese' – was the acclaimed 'BP Recreational Club' which was 'open for membership to all ranks. Rates of subscription, functions, and amenities are all specified in notice exhibited outside this office. Full particulars from Mrs Parker, Club Secretary, Room 33, Main Building.'

'Of course,' says one highly gratified ex-BP worker, 'there was a great cultural life here.' There were concerts and recitals; chamber music classes and operatic evenings; poetry readings and religious meetings;[95] clubs for Scottish country dancing and jazz; language courses, films and lectures; and plays, revues and dances.

There was something for most people: 'My interest was in music. I used to sing.' The 'small choir' of BP workers sang their way though Purcell's *Dido and Aeneas*, Brahms' *Songs of Destiny*, and a new composition – *Songs of Springtime* by E.J. Moeran, a BP RAF worker who 'came to hear us rehearsing his songs'. The wealth of musical talent assembled at BP included professionals: 'Herbert Murrell, a Staff Sergeant here, had his own choral society and was the BBC's Director of Music – they kept him here so he could look after the BBC Symphony Orchestra, at Bedford at the time.'

There were performances too by international artistes, like the pianist Myra Hess[96] and the tenor Peter Pears.[97] One such event saw 'a recital by Pierre Bernac the baritone, accompanied by Francis Poulenc;[98] this was after much of France was liberated'. All who experienced them agreed that 'the concerts were excellent'.

There were also revues: 'Revues took place twice a year [with] sketches and songs – newly written and very funny.' One typical revue, *It's The End, Let's Face It*, staged for eight nights in January 1945, included:

Full cast on stage for the first night finale of 'Combined Ops' - a revue put on by the BP Drama group in early 1945. (BPTA P94/37)

> 'Brush up your suicide – Ibsen, Purcell
> Spamlet or Denmark's omelette dished
> Bulshido, a Japanese sing–song . . .'

Proceeds were in aid of 'The Red Cross & St John's Fund for Prisoner Of War Parcels'. It was characteristic of wartime Britain that everyone was seen to 'do his bit'. Michael Cooper remembered his father, Josh, second in command at BP, dressed up for one revue in his Arab gear 'because he was in Palestine in the 1920s'. Typically inventive of the time were the improvised costumes: 'We had Can-Can dresses made out of blackout material and dyed bandages for coloured frills.'

However, some efforts were not always appreciated:

> 'P is for Parker, the check-suited dope,
> Who thinks that his acting surpasses Bob Hope
> We know that his forté's a bullock's back pins
> Imagine a fan-mail to a father of twins!'

Cast of `By Candlelight`, BP Drama Group November 1945. Left to right: John de Grey, Joan Dudley-Smith, Joyce Dowell, Malcolm Howgill. Photo by Eric de Carteret. (BPTA P417)

For theatrical productions on a higher plane, 'There was an excellent dramatic society with many professional actors and actresses employed at the Park.' The professional talent on show included Anthony Quayle[99] and Bernard Miles.[100] The 'BP Drama Group' itself was a busy and highly organised team. One of their productions, *They Came to a City* by J.B. Priestley, showed their resourceful – and self-consciously dutiful – approach to what was originally only intended as playtime for the workers: 'Material for the set is kindly lent by Bletchley Co-operative Society. . . . To prevent damage to the floor the audience is asked <u>not to smoke</u> in the auditorium. . . . This production is in aid of The Soldiers', Sailors', and Airmen's Families Fund.'

In a demanding schedule in 1944, they performed *French Without Tears* for a five-day run in mid-July followed by Shaw's *Candida* and Shakespeare's *Much Ado About Nothing*. One member of the audience commented: 'Wed 27 Oct – Much Ado in

Cartoon of 'General Wallah' by D. Hukton. (BPTA 21)

the Assembly Hall – Very good!' Members of the group had organised play-readings, auditioned, learned lines, constructed sets, designed lighting, created costumes, found props, memorised moves and cues – all for three substantial productions in a little more than as many months. And it was done in the spare time left after their arduous – and secret – shift-work at BP. Perhaps it acted as a sort of antidote. It was certainly an impressive achievement. They felt so too: 'We put on some pretty good shows.'

But there was no relief it would seem – even in 'leisure time' – from the relentless BP insistence on perfection:

> 'O is for Owen – that's Dudley I mean,
> When the curtain goes up he's not to be seen,
> But if it comes down in quite the wrong place
> It's Dudley the stage boss who loses his face!'

Another important social area was the assembly hall:[101] 'they would have occasional dances . . . We would go out dancing and then go straight on to the night shift!' One young woman recorded wistfully in her diary: 'Wednesday 29th September: Longing to go to a dance . . .'.

There was criticism though of an American dance band sent to entertain BP one Saturday night: 'Their idea of playing dance music was quite different to the English – they didn't have any idea of a waltz.'

One woman who sang with a dance band visiting BP seemed overawed by the experience: 'We were taken in a closed van. We didn't know it was Station X. Everyone was in full evening dress and dicky bows – all the Code Breakers must have been there.'

Such events were organised by one of BPRC's secretaries; before the secrets of 'Station X' were revealed,[102] what follows was his only acknowledgement:

> 'S is for Sedgwick who ran all the hops
> In the tough old days of American cops
> Hush hush, whisper who dare
> He faintly resembles that chap Fred Astaire.'

Other dancing opportunities included the celebrated BP Scottish Country Dancing:

'very well organised and taught by Hugh Foss (known as Lease-Lend Jesus because he went to Washington and had a beard!) . . .'

'He [Foss] had practices during lunch hours, regular dances Friday evenings and more elaborate dances every three or six months with a full dress dance on St Andrew's nights. We wore out his record of Circassion Circle and had a collection to buy him a new one.'

There was also informal teaching: 'The kitchen at BP house was so large that one could dance. During supper break I taught one of the men to waltz. We only had one record – *Sleepy Lagoon*.'

As with theatre and music, dance professionals also visited BP – notably the Ballet Rambert: 'I particularly recall them dancing William Walton's *Façade* when a rather plump ballerina was swung about on her milking stool by two not-very-hefty cowmen. The stage was small and rather low and we who were sitting in the front rows looked in danger of having the Milkmaid dumped in our laps. The fellows in the audience whooped as her billowing skirts blew up over our heads . . .'.

For academic pursuits, one particular Naval Notice[103] was notable for its understatement: 'Anyone spending any length of time here may find the need of some leisure occupation. . . '. In fact, there was a great extent of educational offerings for BP personnel: book loans; correspondence courses 'in nearly all subjects'; language study with Linguaphone records; adult education classes; and the facilities of the Institute of Journalism – 'a professional body, willing to criticise suitable manuscripts'. Courses and lectures also were on offer to all BP staff, including Russian and Latin classes, and 'a lecture by an unshaven unkempt man who looked as though he hadn't slept for a week. . . . He ended up by saying "and that's how I won the Battle of El Alamein". . . . I found out later he was a double agent.'

BPRC offered too the variety of sporting facilities expected of a university – unsurprising perhaps, considering the origins of many staff. There was a badminton court, tennis courts, games room; and clubs for rifle shooting, fencing, as well as chess and cinema: 'I played in a mixed hockey team with Neil Webster – he either hacked your ankles or knocked you about the ears.' In fine weather, enthusiasts organised lunch-hour rounders on the lawn in front of the main building. They included players of international standard:[104] 'It was very informal. As people came out from lunch they joined one side or the other alternately. When there were only a few players the ball had to be hit between two deciduous trees down by the pond. But as the numbers increased, someone would call out "Conifers!" From then onwards the ball could be hit between two conifers more that were widely spaced on either side. We didn't bother very much about keeping the score . . . we just played for fun.'

In winter, the weather might restrict your sporting venue: 'I remember playing an ad hoc hockey game in the corridor.' But the lake might freeze over too for skating, as in one hard winter: 'Some Americans were very good skaters – one in particular, really an expert. I've never seen anything like it.'

The tennis courts drew 'a very high standard from Hut 14' and facilitated other pursuits: 'Someone told me I couldn't sink three pints and cycle round the tennis court three times. I cycled very steadily but the ground came up and hit me on the head.'

Perhaps BP was uniquely blessed with so many varied recreational activities because of its strong 'Oxbridge' base. Young undergraduates and cosmopolitan intellectuals had already experienced the world of specialist fraternities or 'clubs'. It was a way of identifying themselves and their talents – not elitist or alien to them. However, it could also be that BP actively encouraged in-house entertainment to avoid the need for outside stimulation – and its potential danger of indiscretions.

Sybil, Betty, May, Joyce, Hilda, Barbara,
Doris and Mary

request the pleasure of the Company of

MARGARET GODDARD

for the celebration of their

Twenty-First Birthdays

to be held on

Saturday, May 12th, 1945.

Reception 6.30 p.m. for 7 p.m.
at The County Arms
New Bradwell.   R.S.V.P.

Invitation to 21st Birthday celebrations. (BPTA)

'Geese' were highly appreciative of anything that relieved the relentless routine of work and simultaneously bypassed the exigencies of war:

'We posted notices for clothes we wanted to sell, exchange or borrow, if we had a special occasion.'

'Frid 11 June: Unit Dance! Everyone excited. Not much work done. Dashed back, washed, changed, ready by 7! Everyone looking glamorous. Hall crowded. RAF in force – good fun. Excellent buffet & beer. Evening a big success. Lift back in truck. Bed by 1.30-ish.'

'We worked on Christmas Day 1944. One of the men had a bottle of wine and another a Dundee cake. Dorothy supplied home-made fudge and we had a few local cobnuts.[105] Instead of going to the NAAFI for tea-break, we stayed in the office, sang carols, exchanged gifts and had our feast – most enjoyable.'

Christmas celebrations continued even for the boss, as recorded by Commander Denniston[106] in his diary for 1940:

'Dec 24 Our party
Dec 25 Welsford party
Dec 26 Hut 3 Office party
Turkey £1.17s – Presents £2.10s – Drink £6.10s 6d'[107]

Meanwhile, in the BP huts, where work continued throughout the Christmas period, festivities could not be stopped by mere secret war work: 'We had a very small Christmas Tree which the day shift had left, and we hung our gifts on it: razor blades for each of the men and they bought us cords of "Kirby" hair grips – very welcome, to keep our hair above our collars. We exchanged writing paper, envelopes, stamps and pen-nibs.'

But one working Christmas was frenetic: 'Wakened at 7am – opened parcels – hankies and soap. Terrific breakfast – eggs & bacon. To work, on CSM's lap! Crazy day – no work – carols plus American with trombone – 2 o'c service after grand lunch – 3 o'c King's speech – 4 o'c left work. Walked back. Preparations. Dinners 6.30 – grand – tree! – Guests arrived 8-ish – what a herd! & what an evening! Thousands of men & everyone completely mad! Bed by about 1.30am.'

The Christmas parties at No 2 Cottage where 'children of the park' lived were not quite so lavish, but as special. Neville Budd, born in 1938, the youngest child of a BP transport manager recalled: 'the front door was never closed – people who had to work over the holidays were always Welcome. It was a knock on the front door and wander in, get a beer from the barrels set up in the hallway, and then just drink and sing-along to some records, or with Mum playing the piano . . .'.

The Budd children contributed some wonderful anecdotes of living in the Park:[108] 'The whole Park as a playground, climbing trees, collecting duck eggs from the lake, oblivious to the important work of so many people . . .'. They evince the special anarchy characterising childhood – 'waylaying people with snowballs on their return from the canteen . . .' – as well as recall the uniqueness of their situation:

'Playing tag around the back of the mansion, we ventured onto the lawn by the side. It was full of Nissan huts and nude men sunbathing! Horror of horrors – we ran like mad. I don't know who was more surprised.'

'Mum forgetting her pass one day when she went to Bletchley shopping. The guard would not let her in. 'But you know me!' 'Yes, Mrs Budd.' But Dad still had to go and identify her.'

'Being told to keep quiet, always tiptoeing around the house and whenever the phone rang, afraid someone would hear us.'

It was only when the war finished, when they grew up, that they realised their 'norm' had been extraordinary:

'We got used to seeing everyone in uniform – that was how everyone lived. When I first got married to live in a street, I found it very exciting!'

The Lake. (BPTA P.94.15.9)

'The VE service held in front of the Mansion with all the flags was just like a big party. . . . We didn't have to be quiet any more.'

'And then it seemed as if everybody just vanished. We found places that we didn't know existed. We were allowed to go anywhere.'

For older playmates the term *canoodle* is the most explicit romantic expression to be found in BP reminiscences: 'Thursday 17th June: Day off. Bathed etc. . . . Met F. . . . Canoodled[109] on lake.' Euphemisms abound – like 'gentleman caller', 'good fun' and 'things developed' – but not much more to sate the modern appetite for intimate detail. Discretion, the mark of the British persona, was the essence of BP, so perhaps it is unsurprising that descriptions of liaisons were understated: 'We found we had quite a lot in common.'

Always, in the background, was the BP version of 'Big Brother', constantly on the look-out for inappropriate associations. One officer complained that because of a 'confusing lack of hierarchy', COs and NCOs 'fraternised freely in a way that would not have been tolerated at the Army Co-operation Command HQ'. This produced a faintly embarrassing dilemma for one young woman, torn between compromising her secret or her reputation: 'My father, who was at the War Office, would come to see Commander Travis. He'd let me know he was coming and then we'd go off for a walk in the woods. I was a Corporal in the ATS and he was a Brigadier, so it looked quite funny – people wondered what this Brigadier was up to!'

Indeed, BP's surveillance culture resulted in one maintenance worker being severely reprimanded for what he considered an innocent encounter: 'The messengers originally were WAAF girls. We used to play up with them. I nearly got shot I did. I met up with one of them. She was taking documents from the teleprinter room. . . . In half-an-hour I was up the top: "You know you are not supposed to talk to the carriers. Don't deny it – you have been seen." So I said, "I was just asking her when we were going to meet tonight." "Well don't let it happen again."'

The 'Dunkirk spirit' of 'backs against the wall' and 'all pulling together' was in abundance at BP – just as in the First World War when aristocratic ladies organised knitting circles to produce soldiers' socks:

'I helped to start a library. . . . I went to the Library Association to find out where we could get free books. They put me in touch with some organisation that collected books – people handed them in at the Post Office – and we started this Library.'

'Mrs Ridley was the wife of Capt. Ridley in admin. – a formidable personality. . . . She acquired tables and chairs, cups, saucers, an urn and a permit for milk and sugar. She conscripted fellow naval wives as helpers and opened the Coffee Hut. She would pour out the coffee, add the milk and then look fiercely at one and say, Sugar? At first I said, Yes please, then my nerve failed me. . . . I've never taken sugar in coffee since.'

As the years progressed, BP became largely self-sufficient, with its own mortuary, hospital, and fire brigade; but helpers enhanced such facilities: 'Because I had trained at Guy's Hospital, I helped out in BP's Sick Bay. . . . There seemed to be an awful lot of boils and I had to bathe these wretched things. Looking back now, I think they were caused by malnutrition. . . . I would give First Aid lectures during the lunch hour in a hut where they also sold beer.'

The in-house Cinema Club was a further example of BP workers' initiative, created by colleagues 'who were keen on the cinema. . . . We showed things like *Night Mail* and longer fictional pictures as well, borrowed from the British Film Institute. . . . We also saw two captured German films: *Munschausen* and *Prag die Goldene Stadt*.'

At the end of the war some of the BP pressure was released: 'Outside the hut was a great big brass bell – it was more than your life was worth to go near it, let alone touch it. I vowed I would ring it before I left. My chance came on VE night – the whole camp was let loose.' With an end-of-term euphoria, a Wren thus recalled her mischief: 'Quite a lot of us rang that bell. I think the guard officers turned deaf.'

At around the same time, one man who arrived at BP to 'await his demob' found 'a wonderful lot of people' there despite it being 'already run down': 'I made lots of friends. . . . they worked hard and long hours on what must have been very frustrating work. I never at any time heard anyone complain . . . . None would discuss what it was they were doing.'

Even at the end, BP would keep its secrets.

CHAPTER 11

Billets and Beyond

'Ice came out of the taps and there was no heating whatsoever. My room was above the hotel bar and smelled strongly of beer. . . . The ideal was to get to a London theatre and cheer ourselves up, if possible stay the night and come down on the milk train arriving at 5.30am.'

THE BILLETS

'G is for Griffiths who finds us our digs
Some live like princes, some live like pigs
It's no use protesting, you're wasting your breath,
If you find your own billet, he's tickled to death.'

Just suppose . . . you have been formally summoned, with your neighbours, to attend an 'accommodation census' at the local church hall. You must tell the official there exactly what facilities you have in your house – there is no concealing your spare bedroom, or your embarrassment about the outside toilet and the tin bath hanging in the shed. For this is January 1939 and war is looming. You have to do your bit, even if it means opening your door to a complete stranger doing special government work nearby. Duty aside, there is an advantage: the government will pay you about a quarter of your weekly wage for each person you accommodate. And you won't have to provide them with extras like a special sitting-room, or unlimited baths, or more fires, or laundry facilities – you can make additional charges for those. However, if you refuse to lodge them, you will be fined around three months' wages. What do you do?

If, on the other hand, you are one of these special government workers, newly assigned to Bletchley Park, miles away from your home, what is in store for you? You have to go where you are sent. You cannot escape intruding into the personal lives of strangers, disrupting family routines and perhaps their harmony. Only if life for you, or them, becomes intolerable can the arrangement be formally terminated – and recommence with another billet. At least you do not have to bother with direct transactions: payments will be deducted from your BP wages. But you will no doubt approach your prospective billet with some trepidation if you believe unwilling hosts await you: 'People didn't really want you, especially girls, as they left make-up all over the place.'

Before the war, Bletchley was a small, quiet country town, with Fenny

Stratford straddling its north-eastern edge along Watling Street. You could watch fairly contemporary films at its two cinemas. You could find your God at its five denominations of churches and two cemeteries. You could visit its weekly cattle market to buy a live chicken at auction (and pay the auctioneer's assistant *3d* to wring its neck). You could use its railway junction connecting the London–Rugby main line with the Oxford–Cambridge branch. You could enjoy the nearby Grand Junction Canal and the River Ouse. And you could marvel at the silhouettes on its skyline: the gasworks and the brickworks. Bletchley's future as part of the new city of Milton Keynes was only thirty years away, but its buildings now were a hotchpotch of red-brick Victorian terraces, interwar semis, a few thatched cottages, and a string of little lock-up tin shops under the railway bridge ('Tin Town') selling cakes, hats, sweets, fruit, and second-hand furniture.

Among local towns, Bletchley was an obvious location for billets: 'The whole town of Bletchley had been commandeered.[110] We were placed in the house of an elderly lady and her bossy daughter.' Some billets were very convenient for Bletchley Park. Nearly 300 civilians were in hostels within 5 minutes' walk of BP – 30 men in Elmers School and 244 women in Wilton Avenue, just outside the gates:

'We were a very mixed assembly. In the same corridor there was a titled lady and us from the East End.'

'We made many friendships and heard many life stories . . . One sad girl had a baby and hid it in a drawer, dead of course. That meant Police etc.'

The billets lottery might accommodate you at 'Glenhurst' in the High Street with Mrs Cocker; or a 'very pretty thatched cottage in Shenley Road five minutes' walk from the Park'. Other lodgers, however, were not so lucky:

'My landlady was so mean. She complained about me reading in bed and using up electricity with a 40-watt bulb. I disregarded her comments. One night the light went off – she had switched off the mains!'

'I was billeted with the Chief Fire Officer. I had an altercation with his wife who accused me of being an immoral woman because I returned late one night (12.30am) with an officer. She refused to let me in so I had to return to BP.'

'The house was next to the railway line which ran in a cutting just below . . . and was WET. We got wood from a woodyard for a fire in the room and got ticked off. Corporal W went home on leave one weekend leaving a bar of chocolate in her tin hat and when she got back it had been eaten by the mice!'

One Bletchley billet was like 'the Ritz: efficient hot-water system and a good airing cupboard. People came in for baths and brought me piles of nappies to air and dry.' Another was like being part of the family: 'I was billeted with Mr & Mrs Dickens, of Fairfield, Fenny Stratford. They had two small boys, Richard and Joe, to whom I was devoted.'

Bletchley 6th June 1943: The baptism of Valerie Jean Chapman at St Mary's Church. Left to right: John Bosworth with Lady Jean Graham and Florence Brooke (both BP workers); 92-year old Mrs Macburnie and Marjorie Chapman (also BP). Mrs Macburnie ran a billet in Far Bletchley up the Buckingham Road – 'The Orchard' – which had 'plums, gages, blackcurrants, gooseberries, apples and vegetables'. Born ten years into Victoria's reign, she had been a Court Dressmaker for Edward VII and would regale her guests with juicy Royal titbits – as when the King called for his mistress's new gowns. Mrs Macburnie kept open house for BP workers who had been working all night and had missed breakfast. Photo from J.V. Chapman (BPTA P94.13)

The towns of Newport Pagnell to the north and Stony Stratford, north-west on Watling Street, were each about ten miles from Bletchley Park – convenient for BP. Both had ancient coaching inns – The Cock and The Bull in Stony, and The Swan in Newport. And both had old rural businesses that had lasted for generations: Taylor's still sold their famous mustard in stoneware jars in Newport; Hazeldine's the master baker was in Stony; and the Odell brothers – Mr Reg and Mr Cecil – ran their ironmonger shops in both towns.

Although some struck lucky with their accommodation – 'Nice billet in Newport Pagnell. I think he was a bank manager' – it was pretty basic for others:

'My billet was an unfurnished box-room. BP provided a bed, wardrobe, chest of drawers, and a bowl to wash in.'

Stony Stratford High Street, c. 1950 – the A5 Watling Street looking north - showing its two famous old stabling inns, The Cock (left) and The Bull, celebrated in the saying 'Cock and Bull story' and in the nursery rhyme 'Ride a Cock horse'. (LA XSS/ S012)

'You were wakened with a jug of hot water. The loo was outside – if you got caught short in the night there were three doors to negotiate in the dark.'

The nineteenth-century 'new towns' of Wolverton and New Bradwell were built by the LMS Railway Company for railwaymen and their families. Schools, shops, churches, pubs, cemeteries and rows of red-brick terraced houses were all planned and constructed in a geometric pattern of straight streets leading from one of the biggest railway-carriage works in the nation: 'All the little red houses looked the same and were very drab.' The world's largest trams, carrying 100 people at a time, trundled along the Stratford Road. They brought 4,000 men to and from work, fetching their packed lunches from home for them at midday. 'The Works', as it was known, had a loud hooter, the town's alarm clock, announcing when it was time for work (6 a.m.), time for lunch (12 p.m.), and time to leave (5.30 p.m.) – a 54-hour week for the railwaymen. When the Works' gates opened wide at the end of the day, a human river streamed out, dispersing in rivulets down the little streets.

It was a contrast to the 'cultured life of the capital', or the gracious quiet of the Home Counties:

'My accommodation was with the local undertaker. His quaint little wife promised me for my bottom drawer some of the lace doyleys which were used to cover the faces of corpses. I didn't take up the offer.'

New Bradwell from Wolverton Station bridge. (LA XBS/S003)

'I was told that I could have a bath on Mondays but discovered I had to carry upstairs pails of stinking hot sludge from the boiler in which my landlord's railway overalls had been washed . . .'

'The loo at the bottom of the garden shocked me to the core.'

'Mrs M's idea of a good main meal was a tin of pink salmon heated through with mashed potato. We found her a rather moody woman. We borrowed her sewing machine one day – an old fashioned one with an oblong wooden box lid – and out fell all the gin bottles. . . . It was not hard to guess where she obtained her supplies,[111] for next door was a Working Men's Club. At the beginning of each month we'd see her going in there with bags of sweets and cakes . . .'

For the natives however, these worldly strangers could be intimidating: 'A Wren was billeted with my boyfriend's mother. We all went for a drink one evening, although as a factory worker I felt a little inadequate, more so after our shandy – she said she liked "cherry brandy". I did not even know of it.'

There are happy memories too. One recalled being 'billeted with a Southern Irish family who were very good to me.' Another cherishes the memory of 'a small corner shop at the street end . . . I would call in for tobacco – the shop stocked everything.' And one Wren stated: 'I had a wonderful landlady. She was more like a mother to me. They even came all the way to Essex for my wedding in 1945.'

There were thirteen villages in the 1967 designated area of Milton Keynes. Over the next thirty years the new city grew all around them. During the last war,

Dinner time at Wolverton Works, with the world's largest steam tram – ferrying thousands of workers to and from the railway works – in the background, c. 1935. (LA WOW/PO27)

however, they had been untouched, and unconnected except by rural byways, for centuries. Set in gently undulating shire countryside, they showed little sign of belonging to the twentieth century, except perhaps for a 1914–18 War Memorial on the village green. Village billets for BP personnel were varied:

'I was billeted in Milton Keynes village with the vicar and his wife – a <u>heavenly</u> house and heaps of food.'

'I had a pretty hostile reception at the Vicarage, a cold, cheerless house. Later I was placed in an olde-worlde cottage with a couple of spinster sisters. They were so clean, so tidy, and their house so unlived in, and it was equally unfriendly. I then moved in with a chaotic, noisy, Irish household of five and their stable full of horses . . .'

'I shared a cottage in Woughton-on-the-Green – idyllic, beautifully furnished, but an obnoxious landlady inspected our every move.'

'Haversham . . . had absolutely nothing except a minute pub frequented by elderly farm labourers and railwaymen. When we entered, silence fell – everyone glared at these strange middle-class young women who dared to show their faces in THEIR pub . . .'

'In Lathbury Lodge, there was NO gas or electricity. We had oil lamps, cooked on oil heaters and kept warm with paraffin heaters – a coal fire if we got enough coal.'

Further afield included:

> 'a lovely house in Great Brickhill. . . . We never locked it and nothing was ever taken. It was the most peaceful time in the middle of the war.'

> 'a simple little house in Bow Brickhill, a charming little village [with] a sort of "grand lady" who ran things at the church and seemed to impress the locals. . . . The owner was a railwayman who walked along the tracks hammering the blocks between the rails, and cleaned coal from the engines.'

> 'We were billeted in Aspley Guise. The family treated us like dirt – they wouldn't give us baths, wouldn't feed us properly. So we walked out . . .'

The war generated such unprecedented need that even the stately homes of England were not exempt and were requisitioned for service personnel: 'We were quartered in a large house called The Camp at Steeple Claydon. It belonged to Sir Harry Verney and was run by a delightful woman as a very happy household.'

Grandest of all was Woburn Abbey, ten miles east of BP, home to the Dukes of Bedford for 300 years. Set in a 3,000-acre deer-park landscaped by Repton,[112] the

Wrens billeted at Wavendon, c. 1942 (names unknown). Their caps bear the name 'HMS Pembroke V' – the Navy's designation for Bletchley Park. Photo by Eric de Carteret. (BPTA P417.001)

mansion boasted an elegant Grand Staircase, Queen Victoria's own bedroom suite and the famous Long Gallery with its Canalettos and Reynolds portraits:

> 'Woburn Abbey was set in the most beautiful grounds I have ever seen, much to the chagrin of the poor ATS and WAAFs. We suffered quite a lot of jealousy from them. It was rather like a girls' boarding school, so our parents were happy, but they didn't know the ins and outs of it . . .'

> 'I shall never forget the noise of the rutting deer . . . nor that when we came off watch at midnight we all had to climb out of the bus and wipe our feet in disinfectant straw in order to protect the precious herd of deer from foot and mouth disease.'

However, young women had certain other needs: 'Woburn Abbey seldom had hot water and any facilities for drying so all our smalls used to be dried in the racks on Colossus . . .'. Soon, being billeted in a mansion didn't seem so grand: 'The drainage failed, so the water was contaminated. We had to get drinking water from Bletchley. The food was terrible – for breakfast was left-overs from the evening meal, kept for four hours in the oven.'

However, there was one very appreciative and sympathetic guest of Wavendon Manor, about five miles north-east of BP: 'Mrs MC couldn't have been kinder. We were given to the key of the house. There was Daphne the housemaid, Ralph the butler and Mary his wife, the cook. Daphne called us in the morning with tea on a tray with two of the thinnest slices of bread and butter I have ever seen.'

Crawley Grange was 'a beautiful soft red-brick Elizabethan mansion in a remote part of the country' – actually just three miles east of Newport Pagnell. With original Tudor chimney stacks, mullioned windows and a large quince bush by the front, it accommodated around 100 Wrens:

> 'A red nail-varnish line was painted on the bath about four inches up, as a warning that water should not rise above it. We had loos worthy of the house – proper thrones. You had to go up a step with a handle at the side of the platform to pull up. One of them was a cosy two-seater . . .'

> 'We'd play on the grand piano in the ballroom . . . and popular classics on the wind-up gramophone. One memorable evening Frank Lawton and Evelyn Laye[113] came to entertain . . .'

> 'Our cabins were decidedly chilly. We crawled into our bunks with 'Nuffield Nifties' looped round our ears and over our noses. Apparently Lord Nuffield had financed the supply of sanitary towels to the WRNS so this regular supply was put to good use!'

The main army camp servicing BP was the adjacent Shenley Road Military Camp,[114] referred to in many reminiscences – in relation to trying to keep warm and clean, for example:

HRH Princess Royal leaving a maintenance hut – with its somewhat unfortunate notice – followed by Major Haigh at Kedlestone, 1944. From Doreen M. Gibbons née Lovelidge. (BPTA 22)

'The huts were erected so speedily that a roof blew right off in a high wind. And there were no made-up paths, just ploughed-up earth and clay where the bulldozers had cleared the land for hut erection.'

'In each hut there were two primitive iron stoves with tin chimneys. . . . The acrid smoke forced me to pick up my bed and sleep outside in pouring rain – under my gas cape and on my ground sheet.'

'The ablution block had four baths, four showers, and about twenty or so zinc bowls with taps. The loos were urns between two rows of huts.'

Service personnel recall in varying degrees of irritation and fondness the 'ridiculous orders', 'inoculations', 'interminable inspections', and 'absurd' efforts made for VIP visitors: 'The Princess Royal was to visit – bedlam! Unmade paths were concreted in a day so that unsuspecting folk coming off a late shift left permanent footprints like Hollywood stars. Hut floors had to be polished with

HRH Princess Royal inspecting needlework at a Craft Exhibition at Kedlestone with (left to right) Major Haigh, Subaltern Keefe, and Junior Commander Neil. (BPTA 22)

black boot polish until they shone. Coconut matting was laid on all the floors . . . to be whipped away again after the Royal visit.'

A typewritten anonymous circular emerged from within the camp. Entitled 'Going Bush in Bletchley', it described where the 'explorer' could find 'long low huts similar to hen-coops, floored with detachable concrete which rises in clouds of white dust whenever the beds are swept out. . . . The Sports Kit worn by inmates is a brassiere and running shorts.'

The notorious ATS Commander was Mrs Kemp. She tried in vain to impose normal army activities (PT and square-bashing) 'on her rebellious charges who considered that a 9-hour shift at BP was more than enough for one day'. Her particular penchant was to discourage any romantic assignations in the camp: 'The dark lane leading up to the camp was a favourite place for the ATS to bid prolonged goodnights to their current boyfriends. Mrs Kemp instructed the guardroom soldiers to patrol the area and break up the clinches. This was known as the Purity Patrol or "P" patrol.'

A contemporary verse[115] commemorates this:

'MEIN KEMP[116]
The ATS are in my charge, their urges I control
I never let them roam at large without my P Patrol
Chorus
I keep 'em in as much as pos.
On drill, PT and paint.
I make 'em understand I'm boss –
I'm Kemp their chief complaint.

I'm Kemp by day I'm Kemp by night, I'm Kemp from first to last –
My girlies must not ever play, they shall not have a past!
Chorus

The silly children say they think nine hours is quite enough,
But let me tell those idle girls I'm going to treat them rough.
Chorus

Until the war for freedom's won, their freedom will get littler
For in this camp I'll have you know – I'm not Kemp but Hitler.
Chorus'

Nonetheless, perhaps the service life was not as difficult as for one unfortunate soul. Her 'dreadful digs' were so bad that she 'managed to have a carbuncle which had five heads and nearly destroyed the bone in my nose. It was all due to poor diet and dirt.'

TRAVELLING FOR LEISURE

'Bletchley was a marvellous central point for transport. London, Oxford, Cambridge, Peterborough were all easily accessible by rail. The main road was a fruitful source for hitchhiking.'

Within walking distance of BP were the County Cinema on Watling Street in Fenny Stratford and the Studio in Bletchley High Street: 'We tended to walk a lot, go to the pictures, usually surrounded by Italian Prisoners of War who worked on the land.' Aficionados saw such patriotic films as *In Which We Serve* – 'excellent film, but made me think a great deal' – and *Colonel Blimp* – 'Grand!' A visiting American soldier working at BP was not overly impressed: 'I cringed at the American films shown – often tired old westerns or silly comedies. But the natives seemed to enjoy it.'

Some cinema visits ended unexpectedly:

'When I was on ARP evening duty for air raids, there was a very good film on in Bletchley. I was very tempted to break the rules and slip down to the cinema because I felt that if the siren went I'd be able to get back quick enough to carry

Sketch of Hut 130 at RAF Church Green, Bletchley 1944 by D. Hukton. One inmate said:
'We were billeted fairly roughly in a hut which must have been about the size of Hut 3, about
5 minutes from BP, at RAF Church Green. I was in the RAF for 7 years and I don't think I
ever had such miserable quarters as I had here. RAF Church Green was listed as being in
Fighter Command. I don't know how deceived the locals were with that, in spite of the parades
and all that.' (BPTA 21)

out my duties. Having been brought up never to disobey, it was a risky thing to do. I only went as far as the gate when the siren went! I learnt my lesson.'

'Four of us went to see a ghostly film at a cinema that had been built over an old graveyard. When it finished, we went to the "Ladies" – all chatting, not realising the time, when the lights went out. We were in total darkness and shouting "Let us out!" The doors were locked. Someone began playing the organ. . . . By the light left on over the stage we saw the emergency exit and dived at it – absolutely terrified.'

Walking by the canal, or along country lanes, or to a local pub – was the essence of time off work at BP. Friends would have an 'impromptu sing-song' over a drink or 'talk about what each of us would do when demobbed' or bid 'emotional goodbyes when someone's demob did come up'. Special celebrations – like VE Day at the Eight Bells – were generally pub-based: 'With someone's birthday we'd decorate the local pub with bits of hedging. And in the evening we'd all be upstairs having a drink, dancing. . . . It was lovely really.'

The Grand Union Canal at New Bradwell 'where I was billeted, 1944' – from Hilary Pownall née Law. (BPTA P98.1.1)

Cycling took up much of your free time if you explored as far as Bow Brickhill or Woburn: 'A nice little pub at Pottersbury we used to cycle to – the landlady was very good to us – saving little titbits for us poor girls in the services.' You could also cycle to dances held in the camps:

'Most of us had our bicycles. An "all-woman" establishment set in the heart of rural Buckinghamshire surrounded by Army camps and RAF stations – we were in constant demand.'

'We used to go to dances with the American airmen . . . because they had beautiful food and ice-cream.'

For some, the Americans were just too irresistible – and dangerous – a temptation: 'I saw many break-ups of marriages, engagements etc due to girls going with Americans. The girls of course were just as much to blame. I often felt I was missing out when the girls came back talking about the super times they had, and armed with 'Camel' cigarettes, chewing gum, chocolate, etc.'

Cycling 'in all weathers and through the blackouts' had its disadvantages:

'It was quite spooky on those pitch black nights especially going past the timber yard in Simpson Road, Fenny Stratford.'

Cartoon of cyclist by D. Hukton. (from BPTA 21)

'One night I took a short cut by the bridge. I passed someone who stopped me saying my lights were not on and he would have to fine me. I said I'd been working all night but he asked for my name and address. A few days later the summons came. I could pay £1 or go to Court. I had to give away an amethyst bracelet to get the cash.'

However, the biggest advantage of 'getting on your bike' was 'getting away from it all', especially if it was with someone else: 'There were a lot of

Cartoon of bus leaving by D. Hukton. (from BPTA 21)

romances going on. Of course you couldn't actually share a room with a man in a hotel. They asked to see your marriage certificate first. But where you will, you find a way. There was plenty of opportunity for walks in the countryside, bike rides. I can remember drinking champagne on hilltops with young men . . .'.

One of the most memorable images for BP workers was the sight of all the transport – including a fleet of buses and American trucks – lined up waiting at the changeover between shifts to pick up their charges: 'The buses were usually single decker. They had green slatted seats and the springs were made of bricks.' Small notice boards were propped up against the front wheels indicating which villages were serviced by each. One complained: 'We were driven into work by truck, open at the back and the exhaust fumes were dreadful.'

The buses and trucks sometimes provided more profitable journeys, particularly remembered by men:

'Going to the Woburn Abbey dances with the Wrens, alluring in their smart uniforms and black stockings. . . . There would be a barrel of cider on the side and night-lights outside among the rhododendrons.'

'We were 100 American men, at least half of whom worked side by side with the natives, many of them female. In the community at large there was a shortage of men, many of the local lads being away in the service. Consequently Americans were always invited to dances . . . At least half of us were married, but there is little evidence we forgot it. A few of the single men did marry British girls.'

Although 'not many people had personal cars', a van ran to London daily leaving BP at 11 a.m. and returning at about 6 p.m. If seats were available, you could get a free ride: 'I used it once and missed the return journey and spent the night in Broadway buildings, accommodated by telephone exchange staff in their sleeping quarters.'

If you were lucky enough to have your own car, there could still be problems: 'My first car was a Baby Austin. In the winter of 1939–40, we had heavy snow which became rutted then froze solid. I remember driving home through the ruts in thick fog with black-out masks on the headlights and Nora walking in front lighting the verge with her bicycle lamp. I had to shout to her to go more slowly as I couldn't keep up . . . '.

One courting couple commandeered 'the only taxi in town . . . to meet the London train at 1 a.m. or to take us to the many lovely pubs in the area. We gave him a lot of business.'

As ever, the more euphoric reminiscences involve the Americans – and their jeeps:

'Bill, a Captain in the American Signals, drove a Jeep. I was looking at it with great envy – I'd never ridden in a Jeep. He said, Well, jump on! We only drove a short distance when suddenly two Red Caps stood in front and stopped us. Bill said, I'll handle this. He did and we got away with it.'

'The Duke of Kent had been killed and plunged the Air Force into mourning. We unfortunately had planned our very first dance at Wavendon House and suddenly – no partners. An enterprising girl rang the telephone exchange and asked about other officers in the vicinity and struck oil – the Americans had just arrived at Thurleigh. Suggesting 45, they suggested 200! We had our first view of Jeeps – not bothering to use the drive but driving straight over the fields!'

There were two forms of 'travelling for leisure' that most graphically illustrated the socio-economic divide between BP workers. Horse-riding was the pastime of the rich: 'I went riding at Mr Gloster's stables at Newport Pagnell.' For those who were not rich, hitch-hiking was the necessary means of travel: 'We did a lot of hitching in those days . . .'. All the following reminiscences are from women. Firstly the riders:

'My father suddenly gave me a very generous allowance and for one whole season I kept a horse at livery and rode and hunted with the Whaddon Chase . . .'

'While I was at Woburn Abbey I fetched my 3-year-old filly from Scarborough by train. I fed her on brewer's grains and moved her from one thistly home to another.'

'Kitty, an excitable mare, once bolted with the trap, smashing a shop window but emerging unscathed. She belonged to Harold who had a garage at Flitwick and took me on bucolic pub-crawls with the local farmers. . . .'

As for the hitchers:

'Drivers used to feed us on our way up to London. We always tried to flag down a staff car . . .'

'We only had to get on Watling Street and any lorry driver would pick us up. It was perfectly safe in those days.'

'You'd hitch–hike everywhere. I once hitched from Swanage up to Birmingham via Oxford. And then from Hinton-in-the-Hedges home to Llanfyllin. It was easy. You'd get lifts from lorries, service cars. Once I even arrived home on the back of a motor-bike. I'd beat the train if I hitch-hiked home.'

A BP worker could apply for special passes and rates on the railways. There were then around 6,500 passenger stations in the nation[117] and all sorts of journeys, wartime allowing, that one could plan:

'After shift finished at 4pm there was a mad dash to Bletchley Station in the mad hope that the train would not have been delayed by enemy action.'

'When I went home, I left at 9 o'clock, caught the train to North Wales more dead than alive after a night shift but then had two days at home.'

'I used to spend hours in the bookshops – Blackwells in Oxford had a very good second-hand department, and Heffers in Cambridge.'

Commuting from your billet in Bedford could find you in a 'substitute university': 'I recall getting into a splendid compartment with brass lamp fittings that had been resurrected from Edwardian days with a group recruited on their ability to solve the Daily Telegraph crossword in less than five minutes; this duty done, stimulating conversation (not, of course, shop) ensued.'

Bletchley Railway Station portico, c. 1939. (LA BS19)

The Oxford bay at Bletchley station during the war. (LA BS56)

Platform 2 at Bletchley station, July 1948. (LA BS108)

Others preferred to be transported to less cerebral pleasures: 'dancing to Glen Miller in Bedford Corn Exchange and at the Bridge Hotel. My friend Marjorie would sing at his microphone and went out with one of the saxophonists.'

The favourite destination of course was London:

'We went to quite a few restaurants – The Mirabelle, Simpsons, Liberty's, Harrods, Martinez; and for plays we saw *Petrified Forest*, and *Love from Home* at the Phoenix, with an excellent cast. Among the films were *Once upon a Honeymoon* with Ginger Rogers, *The Amazing Mrs Halliday* with Deanna Durbin, *Casablanca*. . . .'

'I saw Margot Fonteyn and remember very vividly some of the National Gallery midday concerts – Myra Hess. So we did quite well culturally.'

The possibilities were endless – even in provincial Northampton: 'A few of us went to hear Joan Hammond in *Madame Butterfly*. . . . The train back was very late. We all took refuge in the waiting room including Joan Hammond who was waiting for the same train. We all got her autograph and she was very chatty and good and friendly company.'

There was a sting in the tail though, and always it came from the burden of duty that weighed on everyday work at BP:

'We would get one day off every three weeks – and anybody who took that day was regarded almost as a traitor for letting the team down.'

CHAPTER 12

The Intercept Stations and Outstations

'The men and women of the 'Y' Service maintain a constant silent watch on the enemies of their country. Their past and continuing contribution to Britain's operational success in peace and war can never be told in full.'[118]

On 17th September 1998, a modest dedication ceremony was performed at the National Arboretum Memorial in Alrewas Forest, Staffordshire for 'members of the Y services whose labours are kept secret and whose efforts cannot be proclaimed'. Throughout their work, it was maintained, 'so many lives were saved, so much achieved, so little acknowledged – for the very best reasons, to preserve the advantage of their very special work' (Lt Col M.K. Hill).

The 'special work' accomplished by the 'Y' service was originally because BP had no direct radio links to receive the coded Enigma messages sent by enemy wireless transmission. 'Y' Stations therefore were set up as a series of listening posts – wireless intercept stations – all over Britain. They sent messages to Bletchley by direct teleprinter line or motorcycle despatch:

'I had no idea all this was going on at Bletchley until I saw it on TV. Then it dawned on me: whatever we took down would have gone there.'

'The motorcycles we used were BSA 500cc, Norton 500cc, and Ariel 350cc. We carried reports back and forth to London daily and to BP – these were very busy days and this work was very important to BP.'

Intercept stations picked up reconnaissance and operational reports – such as on the movements of personnel or supply vessels, and from weather stations and lighthouses. At the hub, and typifying 'Y' operations, was Beaumanor Hall,[119] between Loughborough and Leicester. The intercepted messages received there were sent encrypted to Bletchley Park where they were deciphered and graded on a scale of importance.

One indispensable listening post – the significance of which endures today and where Alan Turing's bicycle would be heard squeaking its way every Tuesday in the early 1940s – was a few miles north of Bletchley at Hanslope Park: 'As the signals from Germany came through, aerials were constantly being shifted. We had a rigging gang to do that. A wild bunch they were . . .! It always amazed me that the aerial poles – 80ft spliced pine trunks – were not buried or anything, just straight on the ground with guy ropes holding them . . . '.

A wireless operator with typical experience of serving with the WRAF in various 'Y' stations throughout the war is Eirlys Jones, a native of Llanfyllin in Powys, Wales. Leading Aircraft Woman (LACW) Jones was 'fired with enthusiasm to join up' when she read *I Was Hitler's Prisoner* by Stefan Lawrence: 'We had to do three months' Morse training at the London Radio School. We got on the London Underground to find it. None of us had been to London before. I don't know how many times we went round on the wrong line. We eventually got off . . .!' Then she was posted to Scarborough, to the castle: 'There was this big wooden door. [To get in] you pulled the string and a great big key came out!'

Her work, along with thousands of others around the country – from Cheadle in Cheshire to Chicksands in Bedfordshire and Flowerdown in Wiltshire – was to search for, and pinpoint, German signals in the vast ocean of radio waves: 'You put your headphones on, and twiddle the knob until you found something. Sometimes you'd hear RT.[120] You'd give the frequency to the sergeant and then they would listen in.' Along with practically everyone else involved, LACW Jones knew nothing about Enigma then: 'It was only years later, relatively recently. We knew they used something special. It would come through in five figures – they'd go on and on and on. You'd get fed-up after a bit.'

Wireless operator LACW Eirlys Jones (front row 4th from left) pictured with members of 26 Group Bomber Command. Others include Sgt Connie Pratt (2nd left front), Flg Off Barrow (3rd right front), Flt Sgt Denise Fraser (2nd right front), and Sgt Peggy Pullen (1st right front). (Courtesy Mrs E. Jones)

Group of Wrens off duty just outside Harrogate. Left to right: Chris Gordon, Helen Sheppard, Kath Coleman, Nancy Hay, Marie Adlam, Renie Ironside, Celia Hepple, Barbara Hicks, Dora Ball. From Marjorie Porley. (BPTA P370.002)

Notwithstanding, she enjoyed time off in a 'very good billet' in Scarborough's Blenheim Terrace: 'Mrs Craig's cooking was . . . well, we put on weight! In our breaks, we'd go to the pictures and Chapel on Sundays – a great big central hall – like Westminster Hall, with tip-up seats.'

Another service-woman also recalled the delights of Scarborough: 'We had a lovely time. We were working with sailors – ask no more. There were dances at the hotel and we put on a little show. A marvellous time we had.' However, LACW Jones was soon moved to Swanage: 'It was better listening nearer to the coast – much more there and clearer. German fighters used to talk like our pilots. They would say "Reise! Reise!" when they were going home – that was their code word for it.'

For over two years, she would leave her 'really good billet – good food and friendly' – to work in one of the Swanage 'Y' station 'igloos': 'They were wooden – one shell inside the other, filled in between with shale from the shore. We had an electric heater to keep us warm – and our flying boots! . . . We only worked with other service personnel – never civilians. Sometimes they'd say, Take the post. And you'd see that one package would have to go to the Air Ministry, another to Headquarters and one to Bletchley Park.'

Then, before the end of the war, LACW Jones was posted to Canterbury, quartered in Kent College 'in a big classroom with six beds – back in barracks! It was all fun except when there was an inspection – there would be a rollicking and then a polish!' Part of the work at Canterbury was:

'[jamming] a frequency set up so they couldn't hear and you couldn't hear and you just kept blithely on. I remember them setting up a ghost station . . .'

'The night before D-Day all the ships were gathering – the next morning, there was no traffic at all.'

Like Eirlys Jones many 'Y' service veterans assert, 'I wouldn't have missed any of it.' A memento of training at the Queen's Parade in Douglas on the Isle of Man recalls a popular melody of the time:

> 'Thanks for the memory,
> Of Derby Castle dances,
> Of Douglas Bay romances,
> And Roger, Roger doesn't mean what everybody fancies . . .'

Another wistfully remembers, after returning late from shift-work, being 'not ready for sleep at midnight. We would have many a discussion – on politics, how our parents had made a mess of things. We even dabbled with a Ouija board.'
A diary kept at Portsdown Hill records more pragmatic actions:

'21.3.41: On arrival <u>No bed linen</u>, only one bed and no room for clothes. Slept in dressing gown and blankets. Beds v hard
27.3.41 Bought stockings, suitcase (invasion), Horlicks tablets, and Oxo for iron rations in my respirator, & turtle oil soap
8.4.41: Bed early as tired. Guns going. Bomb fell just outside garage door on near side of road. I was asleep (2.30) & woke to falling glass & masonry. All our windows gone and ceiling down. Another bomb further down on left. No casualties. Back to bed at 3.30.'

'My posting after training', says another of the 'Y' service 'geese' 'was to Caithness in the far north of Scotland where the station spread out from a tiny village like an octopus – the control hut and five huts where enemy signals were intercepted 24 hours a day.' They would sit 'waiting patiently' for enemy subs and vessels in the area to start radio transmission, then home in on the signal, noting down each coded communication. This was then relayed to 'what we knew as Station X, the name and location so secret that we didn't find out until the war ended'.

THE OUTSTATIONS

'Station X was known to the Outstations as the Nut House . . .'

While the intercept stations of the 'Y' service were collecting the mass of coded messages and dispatching them to BP, there was a huge logistical problem: how could these hundreds of thousands of recorded signals be processed, deciphered, analysed and acted upon without BP actually becoming a 'Nut House'? The solution was in the proliferation of Alan Turing's 'Bombes'. Over two hundred of them were situated at locations within a thirty-mile radius of Bletchley, known as 'Outstations': the nearest were four miles north-east at Wavendon, eight miles north at Gayhurst and ten miles west at Adstock. Further afield were Eastcote and Stanmore just south of Watford on Watling Street. All had machine blocks with only tiny windows at ceiling level, the high walls for deadening the noise and providing bomb-blast protection. Thus, the lack of natural light, and the heat and noise from the machines reproduced the claustrophobic working conditions enjoyed in the BP huts.

One 'Worm's eye view of the war and the bombes at Gayhurst'[121] describes life there thus:

> 'We worked round the clock in two large adjoining huts set in a nearby wood at the back of the house – called B Block. It was an eerie place. You could stand close by the wood and still be unaware that anything was there. . . . There were some 20 machines and each was called after a famous inventor in the field e.g. Volta, Faraday, Joule, Ampere . . .
>
> There were 34 of us on watch – two were duty Wrens to clean out the cloakrooms, make the tea twice during the watch and if it was night watch, make supper – usually bread and cheese.
>
> A Petty Officer in charge sat in the office – in touch with BP by teleprinter and phone. A Leading Wren sat in each room and issued wheel orders – or 'woes' as we called them.'

Others remember Eastcote:

> 'I went to Mill Hill for initial training and then straight to Eastcote and was virtually plonked on the job with the Bombes.'

> 'At Eastcote we weren't allowed to do night shift – women weren't allowed out at night.'

Eastcote was the last outstation to be taken over for BP. At the end of the war, not only the surviving Bombes were gathered there, but also the staff to be retained within GCCS before moving to GCHQ at Cheltenham.

One memory of Adstock – 'a largely Victorian village of brick, partly colour-washed, with some older timber-and-thatch cottages' – describes only basic facilities for their work:

> 'Five Bombes were housed in a stable block, secured by just a bolt and latch on the stable door . . .'

> 'Our food was sent from BP in a large container – cooking facilities were fairly primitive.'

Impressions of the Checking Room at Gayhurst 1943-5, drawn by Helen Rance 50 years later. (BPTA 36)

Much of Lt Col M.K. Hill's address to the dwindling band of 'Y' Service men and women who attended the ceremony at Alrewas Forest in September 1998 could be said of all the 'geese' connected with the work at BP – whether they knew it at the time or not:

'You endured trials other than the occasional fear of military engagement. Your work demanded precision and unfailing accuracy. Concentration could not flag, whatever the conditions, however tired or affected you might be. And when your work was done, there was no chance to relax in others' company – to chat about the work in hand, to air the problems encountered in the conduct of your duties. Most difficult of all perhaps was the requirement to protect your secret knowledge from even your most loved ones. Not just at the time of your involvement but for so long afterwards. No wonder then that another family came to mean so much and to feature so strongly on your lives – the family of colleagues who alone could share your insight into your achievements. . . . This commemorates the whole family.'

CHAPTER 13

Concerns and Regrets

'SECRECY

This may seem a simple matter. It should be. But repeated experience has proved that it is not, even for the cleverest of us; even for the least important. Month after month instances have occurred where workers at BP have been heard casually saying outside BP things that are dangerous. It is not enough to know that you must not hint at these things outside. It must be uppermost in your mind every hour that you talk to outsiders. Even the most trivial-seeming things matter. The enemy does not get his intelligence by great scoops, but from a whisper here, a tiny detail there. Therefore:

DO NOT TALK AT MEALS. There are the waitresses and others who may not be in the know regarding your own particular work.
DO NOT TALK IN THE TRANSPORT. There are the drivers who should not be in the know.
DO NOT TALK TRAVELLING. Indiscretions have been overheard on Bletchley platform. They do not grow less serious further off.
DO NOT TALK IN THE BILLET. Why expect your hosts who are not pledged to secrecy to be more discreet than you, who are?
DO NOT TALK BY YOUR OWN FIRESIDE, whether here or on leave. If you are indiscreet and tell your own folks, they may see no reason why they should not do likewise. They are not in a position to know the consequences and have received no guidance. Moreover, if one day invasion came, as it perfectly well may, Nazi brutality might stop at nothing to wring from those that you care for, secrets that you would give anything, then, to have saved them from knowing. Their only safety will lie in utter ignorance of your work.
BE CAREFUL EVEN IN YOUR HUT. Cleaners and maintenance staff have ears, and are human.

There is nothing to be gained by chatter but the satisfaction of idle vanity, or idle curiosity: there is everything to be lost – the very existence of our work here, the lives of others, even the War itself.
People will always be curious. They can always learn something from your answers, if you answer, even though you only answer 'Yes' or 'No'. Do not suggest, as it is so easy, and so flattering to human vanity, that you are doing

something very important and very 'hush-hush'. Far too many people in England know that about Bletchley Park already. If ever the Germans come to know it, we may find ourselves a German 'Target for To-night'. There are drawbacks to publicity.

The only way, then, is to cut the conversation short. For example:

Question: What are you doing now?

Answer: Working for the Foreign Office (or other Ministry as appropriate)

Question: But what do you *do*?

Answer: Oh – work . . .'

(From a personal security form for all members of GCCS warning against careless talk, issued between 1 and 15 May 1942 (NA ref: HW 14/36))

KEEPING 'MUM'[122]

'The temptation now to 'own up' to our friends and family as to what our work has been is a very real and natural one. It must be resisted absolutely.'[123]

With such forceful reminders, keeping BP's secret from friends and family became an automatic reaction for 'geese', stifling openness and creating subterfuge, even long after the war:

'There were some "ordinary" soldiers who were stationed in the area – quite nice young lads, well behaved, asked what I was doing. I said I was a "telephone operator". That was a good enough reason for going on duty at midnight.'

'One night I was watching Cliff Mitchelmore doing *In Town Tonight* on TV when I said, Good Heavens that's Walter Essinghausen![124] My husband said, How on earth do you know him? Of course I'd never told him what I was doing or who I'd met in the war. . . . Not thinking I said, Oh he was in the Wrens with me. I made some excuse about him being the head of a section or something.'

As a result, some lost the opportunity to share their unique experience with loved ones forever:

'It was sad having to be so secret, because my parents both died, neither of them knowing what I did.'

'The saddest thing for me was that my beloved husband died in 1975 and so he never knew. It became public in 1977.'

But the BP machine needed absolute commitment: one man recounts 'there being almost a mutiny at the end of the War' when colleagues objected to the required work on French intercepts: 'We were lectured about this but there was a definite revulsion about spying on our former allies. . . . So there was nothing for it, if we didn't want to do this, we had to go.'

'Geese' suppressed details of their confidential work for years, having been threatened with 'court-martial', or 'two years' imprisonment' and even 'the penalty of death' for any indiscretion. Small wonder then that:

'It's strange – I want to buy a video of Bletchley Park to send to friends in Australia but still have this feeling I shouldn't do it.'

'I used to be terrified that I would say something in my sleep. There were women who refused operations in case they said something under anaesthetic.'

They 'all took their job very seriously' and felt the weight of responsibility: 'Once I took a Wren friend out to visit relatives. In the middle of tea, she suddenly turned white and left the room taking me with her. She thought she had made an error while on duty. We worked it out on paper and decided all was well. Panic followed while we wondered how to dispose of the secret piece of paper which we burnt in a tiny bowl in the kitchen. My cousins, alarmed by the smell, thought we had gone quite mad.'

Those who were deemed indiscreet met frighteningly unknown ends:

'A philology lecturer at Kings was apparently going to parties in London and bragging about what she was doing . . . I don't know what they did with her.'

'An Austrian girl who worked here was picked up on suspicion of spying. I met her once at a party where she got drunk and started singing the German National anthem. That really got to me, so I told my boss about it, and she disappeared.'

A letter from BP to the Gawcott outstation suggests that recalcitrants were more reasonably handled: 'Sergeant S is in the habit of talking foolishly and perhaps dangerously about his work and implying a knowledge of our work at BP in front of his billeters and others. He appears to be one of those who want to shine before men (and no doubt women). He has bragged about how busy the Middle East battles has made him: "Of course you know all about that at Bletchley etc." Sheer stupidity no doubt but undesirable. If I might suggest it a talking to would do him no harm even if there is not very much in it . . .'.

However, the continuous strain of BP's secret work took its toll. Sleep deprivation (through changing shifts), and nervous exhaustion (through continual pressures to 'get it right') – both were commonplace at BP: 'There was a little convalescent home at Shenley, which was a mile or two away. Quite frequently, people on my watch would have to go there, and I guess I went up there 5 or 6 times. Being pulled back together, sent back and getting on with the job.'

However, with staff absence generally low,[125] it seems that workers would just keep carrying on: 'You'd have nightmares about setting the machines. You'd wake up clutching a phantom drum. The work was painstaking and at times soul-destroying. Depending on shifts, you sometimes didn't see sunlight for days.'

Physical reactions set in with some:

'After two months of night duty I had to give it up as my stomach started going to pieces.'

'I got awful boils by my eye and under my arm . . . the noise of the machines and smell of oil was awful. One of my friends got so run down that eventually she was invalided out.'

One worker realised herself that she had to stop 'because the strain got me down. I realised I could be dangerous because slipping up on one message meant that some agent may be killed. . . . I became afraid to open my mouth in case I gave away something I'd heard during my work. I was becoming a liability. I got ill with the strain of it and decided I should walk before I did any real damage . . .'.

Some workers, allegedly, could take no more:

'I did hear that two people at Bletchley committed suicide as the job got on top of them.'

'People who were not suitable just went and of course other people had breakdowns and they went. I think the writer Angus Wilson had a breakdown when he was here – he tried to commit suicide in the lake and it was hushed up – but then you heard lots of things . . .'

One sad and disturbing case involves an affair between a Park officer and a married Major. As a result of it coming to the attention of BP and Army authorities, the Major was transferred and the woman promptly 'went off her head'. Worried that she would become a security risk, the CO sent her to an asylum in Northampton to ensure she would give nothing away. The officer sent to check on her there was told:

'"No-one must know what goes on at BP. You mustn't tell them. But you must make them understand that she has to be kept by herself so that she can't spill the beans." . . . I went into a grim-looking reception area and stated my business. After a minute or two a man arrived and told me to follow him. We walked along a wide corridor till we came to a barrier of metal railings, stretching up to the ceiling. The man unlocked a gate in them with a key chained to his waist, and after we had passed through he pulled the gate to and it shut with a clang. We walked into a gloomy sort of entrance hall, where several women were sitting in silence on chairs placed against the wall . . . just staring into space or at the ground . . . no expression, not even in their eyes – just completely blank and hopeless. . . . The poor woman was lying in bed with the blankets pulled up to her nose . . . all she did was to sob and say a man's Christian name over and over again. She did not even appear to notice that the doctor and I had come into the room . . .'

The final burden of the war seemed the worst: 'One morning in June 1944, JH beckoned me to a corner and whispered, "We're invading Europe today!" My heart stopped. . . . From then on was a most hectic time for BP.'

For several months before D-Day BP workers were all put on a twenty-mile travel ban: 'This was a miserable restriction, as most of us had nowhere for our weekend off. We were also forbidden to eat at the cafeteria and had to eat in a Nissan hut by ourselves and the food was much worse. Our work intensified under pressure.' But a year later, the frenzy all seemed worthwhile:

'None of us will ever forget 8th May 1945 VE Day: Our work at BP stopped and the machines were silent. We were immediately given two days' leave. I hitched home . . . we got whistled and cheered in the streets because of our uniforms.

> The years that we've spent here together
> Have left us all haggard and worn
> But now that the end is approaching
> We wait with new hope for the dawn
> Typing, typing, Oh for the end of the war, the war
> Typing, typing, we don't want to type any more.'[126]

The celebrations however were overshadowed by what was to be BP's final offensive:

'We assembled on the grass outside the Mansion to hear that war with Germany was over. There was a huge cheer and great excitement – though our delight was muted as we still had the Japanese to finish before we could go home. So back to our decoding machines . . .'

'I came to BP immediately after VE Day and was here for only six weeks . . . Even today I shiver when I remember seeing the message that 'the bomb' had dropped. At that time, I didn't know the name Hiroshima although I did know the name Nagasaki . . .'

'After that' said one Wren, 'I remember having to dismantle the Bombes bit by bit, wire by wire, screw by screw . . .'. To dismantle the Bombes – the source of so much loathing (from its operation) and such elation (from its decoding successes) – was to feel similarly mixed emotions. First the delight of destruction: 'We sat at tables with screwdrivers taking out all the wire contact brushes. It had been a sin to drop a drum but now we were allowed to roll one down the floor of the hut. Whoopee!'

Then came the realisation that BP's special work really was all over: 'It was so strange. It was already nearly empty – a ghost town with just a few removal men shifting furniture. Thousands of people just walked out the gate never to return.'

However, the job in hand – as ever at BP – was paramount, and had to be completed thoroughly. Civil servants were due to come into the Park soon so it was essential that all incriminating evidence of its work was removed. 'We were given plans of the various blocks and huts and an impressive array of keys. An immense quantity of paper was still stored, mainly duplicate signals and we put them in stacks ready to be taken by a lorry for shredding.'

St Mary's Church and cemetery seen through a partly demolished wall of one of BP's huts after the war. (BPTA 94.22.6)

The clearing-up party had nearly finished, when one noticed a crumpled piece of paper wedged in a crack in a wall. Pulling it out she noticed it was, inevitably, 'another incriminating signal'. With the hurried construction of the huts, and the subsequent cold winters 'people had stuffed the cracks with whatever paper came to hand . . . Wearily we went back through all the hundreds of rooms we thought we had cleared and on our hands and knees, or perched on ladders, armed with skewers, we gouged out an incredible amount of crumpled documents.'

All that was left now were empty huts and memories. As one worker put it: 'What was unnerving was when everything stopped so abruptly. It felt as if part of our own being had suddenly died and the mental shock was probably akin to that experienced by a hospital patient following an amputation.'

The silence surrounding their years of work and achievement was to persist in everything 'geese' did for the next thirty years: Even work references were enigmatic: 'Miss A performed her duties in a very satisfactory manner. She was employed on important and highly specialised work of a secret nature. The Official Secrets Acts preclude giving any information in connection with these duties.'

Notwithstanding, there was an assumption that workers' contributions would at least be acknowledged *somewhere*, even if only secretly. However, it was only when some of them revisited the Park many years later that the realisation hit home – nothing had been left, nobody knew of them. Only a small dedicated band of volunteers determined to save the Park was struggling to compile records:

'I note that you have no record of my service at BP. I am somewhat surprised and rather upset . . .'

'I was very disappointed that our section was not portrayed anywhere.'

'Little remains to show where we all spent so much time.'

'It was as if we had never existed, looking at all the displays, searching in vain for some sort of recognition. And talking to all those people and asking about us, I was greeted with looks of incomprehension . . .'

Some 'geese' gave specific reasons why their contributions should have been proclaimed:

'There we were, the very hub of the overseas communications, highly trained operators transmitting and receiving these very vital correspondence and not a sign or word about the part we played . . .'

'The guys that really kept the Bombes running were the engineers. Just imagine what it must have been like trying to trace a fault when everything was wanted yesterday – sometimes 48 hours working on a fault trying to get it fixed and that was right across the board. Technicians were not given credit for what they were doing. We were not the glamour boys, but without us there would have been no end product.'

One of 'the children of the Park' commented dispassionately: 'It was very safe in those days, as everyone knew us, but after, when they were trying to save the Park from being pulled down, nobody seemed to know of us, or of our being there. So that goes to show you how secretive it was.'

Old resentments surfaced in the flow of correspondence that issued after BP's secrecy rules were relaxed:

'Because I was a civilian I did not qualify for the Defence medal – which girls who worked for me did – nor did I receive travel vouchers like them . . .'

'I was a bit of a call-sign expert. . . . My complaint is of course that I didn't get an MBE for that, but the girl who served Milner-Barry who was originally in my section, rather a nice looking girl, she got a DBE. . . . There weren't any decorations if you worked at Bletchley Park.'

Interestingly, what has also developed is an indignant assertiveness unknown in 1940s Britain – 'Perhaps we have kept too quiet all these years . . .' – alongside a sense of pride unusual in the twenty-first century: 'One can be proud to have been a tiny part of it all.'

Common to so many of the 'geese' who have at last begun to 'cackle' is the desire to redress the imbalance of the last half century and give credit where they feel it is due: 'It would be so wonderful if all the wonderful people I worked with in those dark uncertain days could be portrayed and remembered . . .'.

One woman perhaps captures the feeling of 'missing out' in a quotation that could be a metaphor for the experience of many 'geese' at BP: 'Apparently there was a ghost at BP: I never saw it but others said they did in the shadows around the lake.'

Foreign Office,
S.W.1.

30th August, 1945

I have pleasure in stating that   Miss M.B. Goddard

was employed in this Department from   17.5.43

to   the present time   when   her   services were no longer required owing to termination of the work for which   she   had been engaged.

At the conclusion of   her   employment   her   grade was Temporary Woman Clerk Grade II   at a salary of £2.13.6.   a week   (exclusive of war bonus).

During service with this Department   she   performed   her duties   in a very satisfactory manner.

During her service she was employed in important and highly specialised work of a secret nature.   The Official Secrets Acts preclude giving any information in connection with these duties.

Foreign Office letter on the termination of employment of a BP worker. From Margaret Davies née Goddard. (BPTA 17)

Epilogue

'It was a lovely place to be.'
'They were very special years.'
'I feel privileged to have been flung into such a maelstrom.'

Many reminiscences of working at BP exude a sense of wonder – at the nature of the work, at the brilliance of the minds tackling it, at having been involved at all, at having survived it *without* telling the tale. Others, however, wonder more at 'the hell that was Bletchley':

'I could not remember much about Bletchley Park except that from the moment I set foot in it, my greatest wish was to get away from it.'

'Nissan huts, beastly concrete paths, ablutions with rows of lavatories and basins set side by side in a drafty concrete hut – all this brought home to me how much I loathed Bletchley.'

Whatever the judgement, BP moulded the formative years of its workers:

'because I was on my own, really on my own. Not necessarily in with the people who had a similar sort of outlook and backgrounds as at University. But from the actual work that was done.'

'What a tremendous privilege to have spent one's youth at BP – locked into this community with its extraordinary concentration of intellectual and artistic ability . . .'

An American officer perhaps sums up how 'geese' viewed working at BP: 'If you had to be in the Army, it was nice to be in a place where you wouldn't be shot at. . . If you had to have a desk job, it was satisfying to have one you believed was extremely important to the war effort as well as offering a heavy mental challenge. . . . We could be smug in the knowledge that we had been in an important place at a crucial time.'

A British widower perhaps characterises how 'geese' felt about it: 'I have been tidying up my late wife's things. She didn't speak of her time at BP until after various books were published. Even then it was difficult to get her to say anything. . . . Quietly, like many others, she was proud of her work there however small.'

But Michael Cooper's epitaph on his father Josh reflects best not only BP's work ethos, but also its enduring – and sometimes debilitating – effect on the 'geese' who experienced it: 'His was the heroism of the long, hard slog and the burden of ugly, painful secrets, which he carried with him for the rest of his days.'

Notes

BPTA: Bletchley Park Trust Archive
OCEL: *Oxford Companion to English Literature*
OED: *Oxford English Dictionary*
OERD: *Oxford English Reference Dictionary*
OID: *Oxford Illustrated Dictionary*
ORE: *Oxford Reference Encyclopaedia*
LA: Living Archive, Wolverton, Milton Keynes
NA: National Archive, Kew

1   The figures for January 1945 were 3,396 civilians and 5,559 in the armed Services (Navy, RAF and Army). This included 1,963 service personnel at outstations in the region (Adstock, Gayhurst, Stanmore, Eastcote) – total 8,995. (BPTA)

2   From the brochure detailing the sale of Bletchley Park in July 1937. (BPTA)

3   From *Britain's Best Kept Secret*, by Ted Enever, pub. Alan Sutton, 1994.

4   Other SOE (Special Operations Executive) stations included: Station VI: Bride Hall, Wheathampstead, Herts (Marion Hill has also written *The Story of Bride Hall, Its House and Its People*, to be published 2005); Station IX: The Frythe, Welwyn Garden City; Station XI: Gorhambury House, St Albans; Station XII: Aston House near Stevenage; Station XV : The Thatched Barn, Boreham Wood; Station XVII: Brickendonbury near Hertford; Station XVIII: Frogmore Farm, Watton-at-Stone. (NA)

5   Nigel De Grey, an Old Etonian, was a young naval lieutenant cryptographer in the First World War and Director of Medici Galleries between the wars. Became 'a very perceptive and able deputy' to Travis, Head of BP. Retired 1947. (BPTA)

6   Memo dated 27 March 1942, probably from Gp Capt E. Jones, Head of Hut 3 in early 1942. (BPTA)

7   Hugh Rose Foss was recruited between the wars to specialise in the breaking of Japanese ciphers and became Head of Hut 8 at BP. (BPTA)

8   Frederick Victor Freeborn, Head of Hut 7, the Hollerith Machine Tabulating Section, throughout the war. Recruited from BTM Co Letchworth, which produced both Bombes and Hollerith machines for BP. (BPTA)

9   'Hollerith': the punch card system used at Bletchley Park in its early computer analysis of code-breaking. (BPTA)

10 'Devonshire House': the Foreign Office HQ in Piccadilly where many interviews for Station X duties took place. (BPTA)

11 From the minutes of a meeting at Bletchley Park on 23 March 1942. (BPTA)

12 Among the colleges known to have been trawled for recruits was Johnson Secretarial College, London. (BPTA)

13 RDF – later called radar. (BPTA)

14 Brig John Hessell Tiltman, Officer of the King's Own Scottish Borderers from the First World War. Founded military section of GCCS in March 1930 and remained until 1954. Personally responsible for breaking considerable number of codes and ciphers between the wars. Head of Military Section at BP; head of GCCS Research section from its formation in 1941. Deputy Director Mar 1944. Appointed head of the new GCCS Cryptographic group in 1945 – generally acknowledged as the greatest British cryptographer of all time. Died in Hawaii in 1982, but his desk is used to this day by the GCHQ Chief Cryptographer. (BPTA)

15 All four were the most senior officers of BP at the time.

16 Frank Birch: educated at Eton and King's College Cambridge. Fellow and lecturer 1916–1934. Co-compiler of *History of German Navy* with W.F. Clarke. Recruited to 'Sigint' (Signals Intelligence) at the start of the Second World War to head German Naval Sub-section at BP, which was considered 'a law unto itself'. Deputy Director Mar 1944. Appointed head of Historical Section, Jan 1946, and wrote a number of Sigint histories, but died before major work completed. (BPTA)

17 Miss M.V. Moore: Establishment and Finance Officer and Chief Woman Officer; responsible for recruiting civilian personnel for GCCS from at least 1941. Transferred to BP early 1945 to assist in the release of staff. (BPTA)

18   'P5' stood for 'HMS Pembroke V', the Navy's designation for Bletchley Park. (BPTA)

19   Morse Code was devised in the 1830s by Samuel Finley Breese Morse (1791–1872), a pioneer of telegraphy. The code is a telegraphic alphabet in which letters are represented by combinations of short and long electrical contacts, sounds and flashes ('dots and dashes'). It was abandoned as the international call of distress at sea on Wednesday 31st December 1997, being superseded by satellites, global positioning systems, and two-way radios. (ORE)

20   Railway Transport Officer.

21   Capt Edward Hastings RN. (BPTA)

22   Capt Hubert Faulkner, the original purchaser of the Bletchley Park Estate and retained by the government as its site manager. (BPTA)

23   Oscar Oeser. (BPTA)

24   "Bombe" – the name given to an electro-mechanical machine which helped in the breaking of coded messages brought in from the Y stations. Its size was at least 6ft high × 6ft wide and it was devised by Polish code-breakers at the outbreak of war. It developed into the computer of Colossus and proved to be the mechanical bridge between manual codebreaking and the computer age which began with Colossus in late 1943.' (BPTA)

25   'FANY': First Aid Nursing Yeomanry, first instituted in the First World War; became more of a transport service in the Second World War, particularly for secret missions. (OID)

26   Elmers – a nearby secondary school requisitioned as a training school for BP workers. (BPTA)

27   'cipher', 'cypher' – both variant spellings used by BP workers are recognised in OED.

28   'Kafkaesque' – Franz Kafka (1883–1924), Czech novelist whose work is 'characterised by its portrayal of an enigmatic reality where the individual is seen as lonely, perplexed and threatened'. (OERD)

29   *Brave New World* by Aldous Huxley 1932: 'A fable about a world state where human beings . . . learn by methodical conditioning to accept their . . . destiny.' (OCEL)

30   A crib was a message that was repeated by enemy transmitters every day at the same time and on the same frequency – such as weather reports – or it was detected as having a certain 'touch' that interceptors recognised as coming from the same sender. (BPTA)

31   Believed to be the 'Lamson Tube system'. (BPTA)

32   BT stood for 'British Tabulating'. (BPTA)

33   Brown-lead Stationery Office pencils marked 'HB SO War Drawing Pencils Ltd, London 2B'. (BPTA)

34   Herman Hollerith (1860–1929): US engineer who invented a tabulating machine using punched cards for computation, an important precursor of the electronic computer. He founded a company in 1896 that later expanded to become the IBM Corporation. (OERD)

35   4,486 people were recorded working at BP in 1943; 8,995 in 1945. (BPTA)

36   See chapter 12: The Intercept Stations and Outstations.

37   Billeting: placing BP workers in conscripted board and lodging from the local community. (LA)

38   Air Raid Precautions. (ORD)

39   Canteen run by Navy, Army and Air Force Institutes. (OERD)

40   ULTRA: the name given to decrypted messages.

41   Probably Cdr Denniston, see note 106.

42   Author's italics.

43   On this occasion the VIP was Major General F.H.N. Davidson of the War Office.

44   Maj Gen Davidson's letter of thanks stated: 'My dear Travis, I felt I must write you a few lines to express my thanks for the most interesting day I spent at BP, and the very helpful way in which everybody was prepared to answer all my questions. The more I see of your organisation, the more I realise its extent and the necessity for closest touch being maintained between it and the War Office. Thanks for your help and the excellent lunch.' (BPTA)

45   From a contemporary verse composed by an anonymous 'BP' worker, *c*. 1945. (BPTA)

46   Issued to 'all Other Ranks and ATS posted to the Bletchley Park War Site' and signed by Capt G.S. Seabrooke, 25 May 1942. (BPTA)

47   It is difficult to find agreement on what the national average weekly wage was in the war years. The author has created an amalgam of several sources: £3 (or 60 shillings) per week.

48   A call-sign was how operators recognised the sender or location of a message. (BPTA)

49   Hitherto there had been three rotors on the Enigma machine for varying the code. (BPTA)

50   Dispatch Rider. (BPTA)

51   Col H.O'D. Alexander: a child chess prodigy who became an international chess player. Mathematics graduate of King's College Cambridge 1932, taught at Winchester to 1938. Head of Personnel at John Lewis Partnership in London whence he was recruited to BP shortly after outbreak of war. Member of Hut 6; Deputy Head of Hut 8, replacing Turing as head in Nov 1942. Head of Naval Section II (Japan), 1945. Died 1974 aged 65. (BPTA)

52   J.W.R. Herival: former mathematics student at Sidney Sussex College, Cambridge, joined Hut 6

in 1940. Publicly against Churchill's stance on Franco's fascist regime, demanding removal of British Ambassador in Spain, Sir Samuel Hoare. Became head of the 'Newmanry' in June 1945 (see footnote 56 below). Resigned Oct 1945. (BPTA)

53 Maj Edward Rushworth: member of Hut 3 during latter years of war before becoming member of the 'TICOM' organisation (Target Intelligence Committee: see 'Body of Secrets' by James Bamford, 2002). (BPTA)

54 Josip Tito (1892–1980): Yugoslav guerrilla leader after the Germans invaded his country in 1941. He emerged as Head of Government after the war, and though Communist, defied Stalin's authority, establishing Yugoslavia as a non-aligned Communist state and becoming its President for life. (*OERD*)

55 I.J. Good: research mathematician from Jesus College Cambridge recruited via the MOL Central Register in May 1941 – Hut 8 – a 'wondrous arithmetician who never thought but always counted'. Resigned Sep 1945 to take up lecturing post at Manchester University. Later became Professor of Statistics at University of West Virginia, USA. (BPTA)

56 Dr/Prof. M.H.A. Newman: Fellow of St John's College Cambridge, university lecturer in Mathematics and FRS from 1939; recruited for BP Research Section in Autumn of 1942, and tasked with producing mechanical methods to break German enciphered printer. Appointed Head of a centralised research section on special machinery Feb 1943. Commissioned the first machine to process German enciphered printer from Wynn-Williams at the Telecommunications Research Establishment (TRE) in Malvern. This resulted in the 'Robinson', which in turn was replaced by 'Colossus'. Newman's section, was called 'the Newmanry'. Newman left BP in May 1945. (BPTA)

57 Overcoat fashionable in pre-war Britain.

58 N.L. Webster: member of Hut 6 and SIXTA (Hut 6 Traffic Analysis section: 'six-t-a'). (BPTA)

59 Dr L.J. Hooper: Air Ministry civilian who joined GCCS Air Section in July 1938. Head of Italian, later Japanese Air Section. Became Director of GCHQ 1965–73 and was later knighted.

60 P.S. Milner-Barry: international chess player who was also chess correspondent of *The Times*. Student of Trinity College, Cambridge. Joined BP Jan 1940, appointed Deputy Head of Hut 6 Registration Section Mar 1940, then Head. Achieved Deputy Director status in Mar 1944. Left BP in July 1945 for a career in the Treasury. (BPTA)

61 Prof. H.M. Last: Cambridge Professor of Ancient History at Brasenose College, Oxford. Joined BP Air Section as Italian linguist in Sept 1939. (BPTA)

62 S. Wylie: joined Hut 8 in Jan 1941 to found and head the Crib Room. Notable for spotting the tendency for all Enigma wheels on one day to be different from those of the previous day. This aid to Enigma analysis was subsequently known as the 'Wylie WOs' (Wheel Orders). Transferred to Newmanry, then Hut 11, in 1943. President of the BP Drama Group, international hockey player, winner of the Home Guard unarmed combat competition. Compiled 'Wylie's Cryptographers Dictionary'. (BPTA)

63 F.H. Hinsley: history student recruited 1939 from St John's College, Cambridge. ISO (Intelligence Staff Officer) by 1943. PS to Cdr Travis in May 1945. After war, President of St John's College and Professor of International Relations at Cambridge. From 1971 wrote first four volumes of *British Intelligence in the Second World War*. Knighted in 1985. Died of lung cancer in 1998. (BPTA)

64 F.L. Birch: see note 16.

65 Asa Briggs: worked in Hut 6. After war went on to be Vice Chancellor of Sussex University, Provost of Worcester College, Oxford and a life peer. (BPTA)

66 Lt. E.R. Dugmore RNVR officer: joined BP Naval Section in May 1941. Working on French Naval Traffic Analysis by 1942. Head of section by 1943 – transferred to Colombo, 1944. (BPTA)

67 S.L. Newton-John: member of Hut 3. Later transferred to Japanese Air section, deputy to Josh Cooper. By 1945 head of West European Intelligence Section. Renowned for singing, particularly of German songs. Wg Cdr by late 1945. Professor of German at Cambridge and moved to Australia after the war. (BPTA)

68 Olivia Newton-John – star of the film musical *Grease*.

69 Lt Col T. Taylor: US Army Officer and Senior US Rep at BP from mid 1943. Notable US lawyer – member of prosecuting team at War Crimes Trial, 1946. Later became Professor of Law at Columbia University, USA. (BPTA)

70 J.E.S. Cooper: graduate of Brasenose College, Oxford. Joined GCCS 1925. Appointed first Head of Air Section 1936 – a post he held throughout the Second World War as a civilian, regarded as subordinate to Air Ministry. Appointed Chief Cryptographer for Service Sections Mar 1942. Deputy Director Mar 1944, Deputy Head of GCCS under Brig Tiltman, 1945. (BPTA)

71 Based on 'ITMA' (*It's That Man Again*), a popular radio show of the time.

72 Malcolm Bradbury, in the 1958 Penguin edition of *Anglo-Saxon Attitudes*.

73 The artist is Ann Langford-Dent.

74 Letter from 'Maggs at the Air Ministry' to Josh Cooper.

75   'pansy' – contemporary term for homosexual.
76   Section run by Maj R. Tester who joined BP in 1942 from the BBC monitoring station at Caversham. Successful with manual and mathematical techniques of decoding but was convinced that the ultimate solution lay in machinery, e.g. 'Colossus'. (BPTA)
77   Civilian clothes.
78   Also recalled as 'Ann Zupingder'. (BPTA)
79   The Registration Room in Hut 6. (BPTA)
80   W.G. Welchman – 'one of the four people recruited by Churchill to get Bletchley Park going'. Junior Dean and Mathematics Tutor of Sidney Sussex College, Cambridge, joined GCCS in Sept 1939. Head of Hut 6 Registration Section 1940 when Denniston noted he had a gift for planning and organisation. Head of Machine Co-ordination and Development section 1943. Assistant Director of Machines and Mechanical Devices 1944. After the war emigrated to America, where he wrote *The Hut 6 Story* – considered by many as a blatant breach of the Official Secrets Act. Died in 1985 from cancer. (BPTA)
81   Wireless Telegraphy Intelligence.
82   Letter dated 23 March 1941, BPTA HW 14/13.
83   British Tabulating Machines.
84   Meat, sugar and butter had first been rationed in Britain because of wartime shortages in February 1918. Introduced again by the British Government in January 1940, rationing reduced prime elements of the great British breakfast to 4oz butter and 4oz bacon per adult per week. Sugar too was rationed, down to 8oz by the end of the war, by which time allowances of sweets, alcohol, jam, tea, cheese, milk and eggs were also restricted – and remained thus until 1954. (From *The British Century* by Bryan Moynahan).
85   A wartime version of tinned ham produced in the US, immortalised by *Monty Python's Flying Circus* in the 1960s.
86   Where the Americans were billeted, 5 miles SE of Bletchley. (BPTA)
87   Women's Voluntary Service.
88   Fenny Stratford, a nearby village on Watling Street (the A5).
89   Cockney rhyming slang for 'tea'.
90   Hut 2 also eventually housed a small library. It was demolished in 1946 to make way for the car park. (BPTA)
91   Luncheon vouchers – given as part of an employee's pay and exchanged for food at certain restaurants and shops. (OERD)
92   C.H. (Cecil Henry) 'Stoker' Denny, nicknamed due to his pipe smoking. Recruited from Westminster bank in 1942. Became GCCS Finance Officer and later responsible for issuing certain BP domestic items. (BPTA)
93   The Eight Bells.
94   Hut 20 was known in August 1942 to have contained baths and 'ablutions' and Hut 15 was to become *The Bath Hut* by October 1945. Huts 19, 21 and 22 were thought to be additional 'Personnel Support' huts. (BPTA)
95   Hut 12 was used for chamber music classes and orchestral evenings by the BP Music Society; also for religious services for Roman Catholics and Christian Scientists in late 1943. (BPTA)
96   Dame Myra Hess (1890–1965). British pianist noted for her performances of Schumann, Beethoven, Mozart and Bach, and for her piano transcriptions of Baroque music. Her lunchtime recitals in London's National Gallery were highly acclaimed as morale boosters during the war. (ORE)
97   Sir Peter Pears (1910–86), known as Benjamin Britten's partner, was celebrated as having created the title roles in most of Britten's operas, notably *Peter Grimes* (1945). With Britten he founded the annual Aldeburgh Festival from 1948. (ORE)
98   Francis Poulenc (1899–1963), a noted French composer who wrote sonatas for flute, oboe and piano, the ballet *Les Fiche*, an opera *Dialogues des Carmelites* and many songs. (ORE)
99   Sir Antony Quayle (1913–89), British actor famous for his film roles in *Lawrence of Arabia*, *The Battle of the River Plate* and *The Guns of Navarone*; and for his theatre roles in *Antony and Cleopatra* and *Othello*. (ORE)
100   Bernard Miles, Baron (1907–91): British actor-producer, noted for his performances in films such as *Great Expectations* (1947), and for founding a Trust which built the City of London's first theatre for 300 years, The Mermaid, which opened in 1959 with the musical play *Lock Up Your Daughters*. (ORE)
101   Wilton Hall, 'near the canteen' – purpose-built for BPRC, continued after the war as a ballroom, cinema, theatre and cabaret venue; and in the 1960s it was host to rock bands like The Who and The Rolling Stones. Recently refurbished, it is still hired out for weddings, summer balls, dinner dances, banquets, fashion shows, and 'multimedia corporate presentations'. (LA)
102   See *Station X*, by Michael Smith, pp. 81–2
103   'Naval Notice No 41, 2nd October 1944: Facilities for Education and Mental Recreation – Naval Personnel'. (BPTA)
104   Hugh Alexander and Gordon Welchman.
105   Hazelnuts.
106   Cdr Alistair Graham Denniston, 'the little man': Head of GCCS from 1919 and of BP until 1941

when he was replaced by Cdr Edward Travis. (BPTA)

107 The money spent was the equivalent of half a month's average salary. (LA)

108 The four siblings were Robert ('Bobby', 1924–2000), twins Jean and Faye (born 1934, now Jean Cheshire and Faye Barnwell) and Neville ('Nev', born 1938). (BPTA)

109 'slang. orig. US, to indulge in caresses and fondling endearments', from the *OED*.

110 An 'Important Government Notice' issued in October 1941 to 'the Owner or Occupier of any Dwelling House in Bletchley' gave details of an Order made by the Ministry of Health: 'In order that accommodation may be reserved for persons who will need to be brought into Bletchley for work of essential national importance, the Government have decided that it is necessary to place restrictions on the numbers of people who may come into the district . . . You will not be able to allow any person to stay at your house for more than three consecutive nights . . . without the consent in writing of the Lodging Restrictions Appeals Committee of the Urban District Council . . . [unless] you are required to take persons in by a billeting notice . . . '. (BPTA)

111 Alcohol was rationed during the war, as were sweets and cakes. Swapping was commonplace. (LA)

112 Humphrey Repton (1752–1818), British landscape gardener. (ORE)

113 Evelyn Laye was married to Frank Lawton – they were musical comedy stars of the time. (ORE)

114 In January 1945, 364 Army men and 341 ATS women were recorded at the camp. (BPTA)

115 Composed and performed, it is believed, at the final Christmas concert in 1944. (BPTA)

116 A pun on *Mein Kampf*, Adolf Hitler's autobiography.

117 The Beeching Report of 1963 recommended swingeing cuts to the nationalised railway system:

a third of the total number of stations in 1948 were closed. (ORE)

118 Lady Martin, WRN Bletchley Park, at Alrewas Memorial Service, 1998. (BPTA)

119 Once the stately home for the Herrick family, Beaumanor was requisitioned by the War Department in 1939 as one of the best areas to receive German High Frequency radio signals and became the headquarters of the War Office 'Y' Service. Its extensive grounds were covered with a huge system of 'dipoles', 'rhombic antennas' and huts filled with banks of receivers, many of them cunningly camouflaged – for example as cricket pavilions – to confuse both local villagers and German reconnaissance flights. (BPTA)

120 Radiotelegraphy.

121 Written by Marion Hughes (wife of Labour MP for Newham East), sent to Liam Fox, and now in the BP Archives. (BPTA)

122 A Government wartime propaganda notice of the time urged discretion with 'Keep Mum, she's not so dumb!' (BPTA)

123 The conclusion of a Special Order to BP staff from Cdr Travis to mark VE day. (BPTA)

124 The reminiscence continued: 'I remember Walter Essinghausen as an extremely nice man, short and stocky, very dark hair, very kind and everybody liked him immensely. I didn't realise until I read the book *Codebreakers* – in which he wrote two chapters – that he was a German Jew. He said he could only assume that when he was interviewed for the job whilst at Oxford, they realised he had more incentive than most to want to defeat Hitler. He went back to Israel after the war and was Minister for Foreign Affairs.' (BPTA)

125 Recorded at only 5 per cent in January 1945. (BPTA)

126 From 'The Swan Song' of GBR (German Book Room), to the tune of 'My bonnie lies over the ocean'. (BPTA)

Sources and Acknowledgements

FROM THE BLETCHLEY PARK TRUST ARCHIVES

AMBLER: Avis Ambler
ANDERSON: Wendy Munro née Anderson
ATKINS: Mr Atkins
ATKINSON: Dorothy Atkinson
AUSTERFIELD: Eric S. Austerfield
AXON: Alice Mitchell née Axon
BARBER: Doris Walker née Barber
BAKER: Bob Baker
BARNES: Joan Collins née Barnes
BARRATT: Russell Barratt
BARRETT: Arthur Barrett, re Joan Barrett née Molliex
BARTON: Audrey Barton
BATEY: Mavis Batey
BEARMAN: Mrs J.E.A. Noakes née Bearman
BERRIMAN: Mary Rock née Berriman
BIGGS: Bob Biggs
BLOOM: Margaret Thomas née Bunny Bloom
BOWRING: John Bowring
BOYCE: Pauline M. Boyce
BRETTELL: June Brettell
BREWSTER: Molly Brewster
BRIGGS: Ernie Briggs
BROCKLESBY: Mary B. Parker née Brocklesby
BUDD: Faye Barnwell née Budd
BUDD: Jean Cheshire née Budd
BUDD: Neville Budd
BUDD: Robert Budd
BURKITT: Patricia E. Rumpf (Pat Hyman) née Burkitt
BURROW: Pauline Lee née Burrow
CASSAR: Joseph Cassar MBE BSc
CAUGHEY: Catherine M. Caughey
CHAPMAN: F/Lt J. Vincent Chapman
CHARNIER: S/O Wendy Jay née Charnier
CHERRINGTON: Ruth Isabel Ross née Cherrington
CLIFFE: Joyce Thompson née Cliffe

COLLINS: Charles Collins
COLLINS: Tom Collins
COLES: Phyllis Coles
CONLAN: Francesca (Frankie) Webber née Conlan
COOK: Collette Cook
COOKE: Barbara Cooke
COOPER: Michael Cooper
COOPER: Bess Farrow née Cooper
CORNWALL-JONES: M. Cornwall-Jones
CROFT: John Croft
DEACON: Betty Hill née Deacon
DEACON: Elaine Baly née Deacon
DEWAR: Betty Johnson née Dewar
DOUCH: Mrs Gwen Douch
DRING: Deidre Capron née Dring
DRUCE: Miss Francis Druce
EGINGTON: June Douglas, née Egington
ELLIS: Roy Ellis
FARADAY-DAVIES: Jean Wallwork née Faraday-Davies
FARMER: Dennis Farmer
FARMER: Pat Farmer
FARR: Mavis Faunch née Farr
FELLOWS; Mrs Gwen Morley-Mower née Fellows
FINEDON: F.H. Finedon
FREER: Stephen Freer
GALLILEE: Muriel (Mimi) Gallilee
GEORGE: Eric George
GIBBONS: Ron Gibbons
GODDARD: Margaret Davies née Goddard
GOODCHILD: Mrs G.L. Muir née Goodchild
GOODMAN: Raymond Goodman (founder of *Which?* magazine in 1950)
GRAHAM: Ann Witherbird née Graham
GRANT: Neil Grant
GREENFORCE: WRNS Greenforce

HANSFORD: Elizabeth Persival, née Bettina Hansford
HARPER: LACW H. Bragg née Harper
HARRISON: Kay Pickett née Harrison
HAWKEN: Elizabeth Hawken
HAWKES: D.R. Hawkes
HEAL: Sheila R. Heal
HERIVAL: John Herival
HOOD: Ann Finding née Hood
HOWKINS: Peter Howkins
HUGHES: Marion Hughes
HUKTON: D. Hukton
HUNTER: Doris Heaney née Hunter
HYMERS: Winifred Ribchester née Hymers
JONES: LACW Eirlys Jones
JONES: Joyce Stevens née Jones
JULIUS: Diane Cooper née Julius
KEELING: Alan (Richard) Keeling
KENT: LACW Kent
KIDMAN: Joan Allen née Kidman
KINGSLEY-LARK: Irene Thrupp née Kingsley-Lark
LANCASTER: Sheila Lancaster
LANGFORD DENT: Ann Langford Dent
LAW: Hilary Pownall née Law
LAWN: Oliver Lawn
LAWRENCE: Daisy E. Lawrence (Lawrie)
LAWRY: Beryll Lawry
LEASK: Mrs Diane K. Leask
LeBLOND: Marie Bennett née LeBlond
LLOYD: Ben Lloyd
LOVELIDGE: Doreen Gibbons née Lovelidge
LUKE: Doreen Luke
LUSHER-PENTNEY: Marjorie Chapman née Lusher-Pentney
MACKENZIE: Sheila Lawn née Mackenzie

MacLENNAN: Morag Beattie née MacLennan
McCARTHY: Eileen Moore née McCarthy
McNEELY: Margot McNeely
MEADOWS: Anne Ross née Meadows
MEDHURST: Rozanne Colchester, née Medhurst
MONKTON: H. Monkton
MOORE: Marjory Campbell née Moore
MOORE: Mavis Cannon née Moore
MYERS: Ken Myers
NORTON: Sarah Baring née Norton
O'DONAHUE: Pamela O'Donahue
OSWALD: Daphne Burton née Oswald
PAGE: Gwendoline Page
PAWLEY: Margaret Pawley
PAYNE: Diana Payne
PEASE: Anne Chetwin-Stapleton née Pease
PEARSON: Irene Pearson
PEMBERTON: Dorothy Roscoe née Pemberton
PHILLIPS: Naomi Holme née Phillips
PRESTON: Gordon Preston
RAE: Mary Rae
RANCE: Helen Rance
REID-TODD: Margaret Stephens

née Reid-Todd
RICE: Jean Rice
RICHARDS: F.L. Duggan née Richards
ROBERTS: Ruth Roberts
ROBINSON: Joyce Rushworth née Robinson
ROCKET: Stephen Rocket
ROSS: Margaret Ross
RUSSELL: Anne Russell
SANDISON: Isabel F. White née Sandison
SCRIMGEOUR: Daphne Scrimgeour
SEDGWICK: Stanley Sedgwick
SHARP: Walter Sharp
SKEVINGTON: Malcolm Skevington
SKINNER: Peggy Skinner
SMITH: Muriel Winter née Smith
SMITH: Pauline Powell née Smith
SMITH: Peter J. Smith
SPENCE: Diana Neil née Spence
SPENCER: Doreen Luke née Spencer
STEVENSON: Joan Brown née Stevenson
STEWART: Rena Stewart
STONES: Beryl Warrington née Stones
SWATTON: Mr H.L. Swatton

SWEETLAND: Gladys E. Sweetland
TERRY: Jay Terry
THIRSK: James Wood Thirsk
TOLLETT: Joan Marr née Tollett
TUCKER: Barbara Hart née Tucker
TYLER: Diana Lauder née Tyler
VALENTINE: Jean Valentine
VANCE: Helen Vance
VERNHAM: Deone Bartlet née Vernham
WALLS: Doris Calvert née Walls
WARNER: Margaret Stidham née Warner
WATKINS: Joan Thirsk née Watkins
WATSON: Bob Watson
WEST: Caroline Shearer née West
WHITE: Beryl Paige née White
WHITE: Isabel White
WHITE: Doris White
WHITING: Margaret Martin née Whiting
WHITING: Olive E. Keppel-Powis née Whiting
WILDEY: Beryl Robertson née Wildey
WILLIAMSON: Ann Mitchell née Williamson
WISE: Nan Wise
WITHERBIRD: Arthur Witherbird
WOOKEY: Joan Wookey
WRIGHT: Mrs I. Wright

FROM SOURCES HELD AT THE IMPERIAL WAR MUSEUM

Individual memoirs:
ADAMS: Mrs P.N. Adams
LEASK: Mrs Diane Leask
OWEN: Mrs Gwendolen Peck née Owen
WILKINSON: Mrs Audrey Webster née Wilkinson

Verbatim extracts from the portfolio collected by Mrs M.W. Ackroyd:
CHAPPELL: Mrs Pat Harrowing née Chappell
GARRETT: Mrs Imogen Ryan née Garrett
GEDDES: Mrs Rosemary Morton née Geddes
HALE: Miss Gay Hale
HOWARTH: Mrs Joan Russell née Howarth

HUMPHRYS: Mrs Daphne Baker née Humphrys
JABEZ-SMITH: Mrs Vivienne Alford née Jabez-Smith
LYSTER: Rosemary Lyster
ROBERTSON: Mrs Dorothy Smith née Robertson
SCAMELL: June N. Loye née Scamell

Extracts from the unpublished MS of Eric Rhodes for 'Ladies of the Park':
BLAKE: Miss Gladys M. Blake
CASSIDY: Mrs Dorothy Cassidy
CLARK: Mrs F.E. Clark
DOBSON: Mrs Olive J. McGrivy née Dobson
DRIVER: Mrs Mary Ferguson née Driver

DUDLEY-SMITH: Mrs J. Dudley-Smith
HOLLIDAY: Mrs L.P. Holliday
JACKSON: Mrs Marjorie Pearson née Jackson
LIDDLE: Mrs S. Liddle
MARRIOT: Mrs Winifred E. Marriot
McLAUGHLIN: Mary S. McLaughlin
PARTRIDGE: Mrs Barbara L. Partridge
PERKINS: Mrs Joan Perkins
SHEARGOLD: Kay Sheargold
SIMPSON: Mrs Jean Simpson
TOOLEY: Mrs Molly Eason née Tooley
WARD: Mrs M. Ward
YOUNG: Mrs Dorothy M. Barlow née Young

BIBLIOGRAPHY

Ashford, D. (ed.), *In Search of the Leons*, by students of Leon School, Milton Keynes
Caughey, Catherine M., *Breaking the Code*
Enever, Ted, *Britain's Best Kept Secret*, 1991
Grant, Clare, article in *The Mirror*, 22 August 2001
Hinsley, F.H. and Alan Stripp, *Code Breakers*, 1993
Markham, Sir Frank, *The History of Milton Keynes and District*, 1973
Smith, Michael, *Station X*, 1998

ACKNOWLEDGEMENTS

The author is very grateful for the help and support of staff at: The Bletchley Park Trust Archive, particularly Alex Scott; the Living Archive in Wolverton, and Bletchley, Milton Keynes, particularly Zena Flinn and Tracy Whitmore; the Imperial War Museum; and the National Archive at Kew; and especially Doris Hill and Bob Hill.